THE AUTOBIOGRAPHY OF AN ENGLISHMAN

THE AUTOBIOGRAPHY OF AN ENGLISHMAN

'Y'

Paul Elek
LONDON

FIRST PUBLISHED IN GREAT BRITAIN 1975
BY ELEK BOOKS LIMITED,
54–58 CALEDONIAN ROAD,
LONDON N1 9RN

ISBN 0 236 31085 2

MADE AND PRINTED IN GREAT BRITAIN BY
THE GARDEN CITY PRESS LIMITED
LETCHWORTH, HERTFORDSHIRE SG6 1JS

PREFACE

This is the life-history of an Englishman now in his sixties. It concentrates on what he calls the 'secret strand', that is the emotional and sexual part of his life which his upbringing and habits of mind have led him to keep concealed. Y prefers to remain anonymous for private and personal reasons. Possibly some of the guilt that he associated with his private proclivities at an early age remains with him in a residual form despite the changes in mores and emphases that have occurred over the past decade or so. He has altered only the names and other factual circumstances in his life that could reveal his identity to those who know him well. In all essentials, in all the details of private acts and thoughts and personal relationships, the account is authentic. If it had been fictionalised to even a slight extent it would not have satisfied Y's need to put down on paper and so come to terms with the facts of his inner life. Y is a well-known writer and critic.

I made Y's acquaintance in the course of my professional work when he came under my care for certain emotional complaints not unconnected with the circumstances described in this book. He asked me to read his manuscript in order to gain understanding of his clinical problems. On reading it I realised at once that here was an important revelation of an individual's sexual complexities, told with a frankness and honesty rarely shown by writers of fiction, biographers and certain confessional authors now in vogue. I suggested to Y that his document ought to be published.

Y's story is very typical of many an Englishman of his own age who underwent similar ambiguities in sexual development. He was brought up in a liberal-non-conformist home by parents at once benevolent and remote, and educated at a boys' preparatory and public school. The stage was set for those inevitable conflicts in sexuality that bewilder many intelligent and sensitive boys. Y experienced all the pleasures and pains physical and psychic of a schoolboy and formed strong emotive attachments to boys before emerging at Cambridge and then into the wider English adult world where sexual conventions were satisfied by heterosexuality, marriage and parenthood. Experiencing a satisfactory marital relationship for a while, Y went on to form a liaison with a girl much younger than himself, who helped him to mature the sexuality that seemed to have been hampered by his upbringing.

The death of his wife was the great strain that caused total collapse of what appeared to have been strong heterosexual relationships. Following his wife's death and while Y was still very attached to his family and children he fell back upon supportive emotive attachments with persons of his own sex. Clearly Y was sustained subsequently by these homosexual relationships and was able to function as a fairly normal integrated individual once more.

Y's story would indicate that bisexuality is widely experienced. Similarly Y makes no bones about the gratifications he obtained through sado-masochistic practices as a schoolboy, and later in those conflicts surrounding his frustrating love affairs both hetero- and homosexual. The most striking and valuable lesson to be learned from Y's experience is that the crucial feature about the relationship between two people, whether of the opposite or the same sex, is the emotion, and physical contact, of love. The sexual objects of this emotion are readily interchangeable depending on upbringing, circumstances and life-crises.

In my own clinical practice as a psychiatrist I have derived considerable value from the use of Y's text as an authentic case-history. Both its clinical usefulness and its appeal to the general reader lie in its being a completely truthful human statement.

S. Jacobson

I

My first love affair was with a boy named Ian. We were both about ten, he perhaps slightly the younger. We were in our first term at our first boarding school and both of us were homesick, scared and in need of mutual consolation. The school, Yattonbeck, was a Quaker foundation run by dedicated and high-minded men and women who believed in freedom and knew little of what went on among the pupils. What went on in my case was severe persecution—on account of my oddness. Till then I had not been in any way conscious of this oddness. The school was in the North, and I spoke with a Southern accent. I also wore spectacles, which were not nearly so common among children in those days as they have since become. There were some decent boys in the school, whose friendship and protection I sought, but in the permissive atmosphere prevailing they had little power to restrain the rougher elements, whose butt and victim I became. The persecution was trivial but to an impressionable boy overwhelming. I was bullied in the dormitory, in the lavatories, on the playing-fields. I hated the place and dreaded the beginning of each term. I was not by nature a sensitive plant, but Yattonbeck turned me into one.

The school was nominally co-educational. Boys and girls shared lessons and meals together, but inhabited separate blocks and used separate playgrounds. The girls victimised me more bitterly and spitefully than the boys. The co-educational principle was established by allowing boys and girls to walk round and round the boys' playground together for an hour before lunch every Sunday. I was invited by the sister of my closest friend—not Ian but an older boy—to partner her in this parade. I refused, as I had no interest in her and was scared of girls.

My relationship with Ian was probably the only purely innocent love affair I have ever had. It was mutual from the start. We drifted together; I don't know which of us took the initiative. We were allowed to go on walks, in company with at least one of our own sex, on Sunday afternoons. We spent our weekly eightpences in the village on sweets and pork pies (food just after the First World War was inadequate and unpalatable) and then set off, always to the same spot—a cave we had made for ourselves under some pine trees near the edge of the wood. Absolute seclusion was all we sought. Here we would settle down, enjoy our tuck, and then lie down with our arms around each other. We kissed, but had no closer physical contact.

Ian had the particular type of face that has always attracted me. I believe many, perhaps most people are drawn to some such face or personality. There is often, I have noticed a marked physical resemblance between the different objects of a person's desire. Ian had a perfectly clear, pink and white girl's complexion, soft grey eyes with long lashes and dark hair. But more than all this he had the bone structure that has always appealed to me—high cheekbones and an oval, somewhat pointed face, with a slightly tiptilted nose, a smooth brow and a delicately curved mouth, neither very full nor very sensual. Such is the face of almost everyone I have desired—my first serious girl love, my wife, and others, male and female. The Vermeer girl's head has something of this look. The length and proportion of the face and the high cheekbones give the face a gravely mournful appearance, suggestive of something remote and unobtainable. The shape is all-important, but so also are the clearness and surface perfection of the skin. No one with a muddy skin has ever attracted me. The tactile quality is essential. There is also, about this cast of face, a sort of chasteness which has nothing to do with chastity.

As I kissed Ian's face, shyly but with no shame, I remarked one day, laughing, 'Fancy kissing Kevin!'

Kevin was the boy whom Ian had come to school with at the beginning of his first term. He was from Belfast. He had a sister who one day savagely and bitterly attacked me for having separated her brother from his friend Ian. I could only deny the accusation since I had acted quite innocently, and the attraction between Ian and me was immediate and instinctive. But Kevin's sister was perhaps right, at a subconscious level.

I don't know how long the affair with Ian lasted. We never spoke of it to anyone else, not from fear or shame, but simply because such things were not spoken of. Our love was a wild flower in a desert of misery and petty persecution. We certainly never quarrelled. The thing ended, as I imagine such things always do, when our interests were engaged elsewhere. I may simply have dropped Ian when I formed an intellectual friendship with Maurice, an older boy, who was the son of a science teacher at the school. It was his sister who had invited me to 'walk round'. We shared literary interests and read together the writings of Stephen Leacock, for whose humour we had an inordinate admiration. Although Maurice was several years older than I, I don't think he had any emotional interest in me. I had none in him, and I have never been sexually attracted to anyone older than myself, male or female. Maurice was evidently obsessed with the problems of puberty, for he was my first instructor in the pleasures of masturbation, though on a strictly theoretical basis. What he told me was that a wonderful sensation could be had from playing with one's penis. I had never been consciously aware of this before, and I remember storing the knowledge in my mind for future investigation. I was not ready for masturbation, and Maurice did no more than tell me about it. Yet for years I bore him a grudge for having imparted this forbidden knowledge. Even in theory it became a secret with which my mind was haunted, so that from the first masturbation was associated with secrecy and guilt. When Maurice told me of the feeling that accompanied masturbation, I tried to help him out by putting it into words. Pure guesswork on my part, of course.

'You mean,' I said, 'a feeling of the joy of life?'

'That's it,' he agreed.

It was not till long after I had left Yattonbeck that I first masturbated. It was at home, and I had changed into tennis clothes. I must have been thirteen or so, I don't remember. It was a warm summer afternoon, and the sun made me feel drowsy and sensuous. Feeling my penis excited by the warmth, I began to rub it, at first gently and then more excitedly with my hand. In a few minutes the climax came. The feeling of release was enormous, but the sense of panic, fear and guilt was even greater. The actual ejaculation frightened me, and I was certain I had done myself some irreparable harm. That a boy's loss of innocence should occur like this, instead of with a girl, has always seemed to me tragic, in that it automatically increases his sense of isolation and gives him the feeling that true gratification is only to be sought in and through himself. I had no previous knowledge of the facts of sex, though I remember that my father had once tried to tell me. However, he was hesitant and nervous, and I had not the confidence in him to help me ask questions. What he warned me about was, in fact, wet dreams, which have nothing to do with masturbation, except that they occur most frequently with non-masturbators who have no other outlet for sexual potency.

After this crucial experience I made myself a promise never to masturbate again. It was four days later, this time in the lavatory, that I masturbated for the second time. After that masturbation became habitual, thus, as it were, closing the circle of my isolation, guilt and misery, in a never-ending dreary round. I certainly enjoyed it, as I infrequently still do, and always with a sense of guilt, shame and despair. We never spoke of it at school, and I think it was everyone's guilty secret. I think now that I did not start until later than thirteen—perhaps I was fourteen—for I was that age when I left my prep school for a public school, and at the former masturbation did not figure in our lives at all. Sexual excitement at my prep school was in fact associated, not with masturbation but with flagellation.

I can't recollect evidence of sexuality before I went to Yattonbeck at the age of nine or ten, but the pattern of my hidden life was being set long before then. Anyone looking at certain early photos of me would label them 'portrait of a prig'. My hair was smarmed down with water and my neck surrounded by an Eton collar. Other photos give an appearance of spontaneous merriment, of which there was plenty in our house.

To anyone who has not lived it, it is impossible to give a clear picture of middle-class home life in a chapel-going family. My parents were well-to-do, though not rich. They believed in education and in the value of social superiority. They were not consciously snobs, but they had definite ideas on how not to offend people and how to avoid too close contact with social inferiors. Plain living and high thinking was no cliché—it was the reality in our family. We went to chapel each Sunday and were more or less sabbatarian. We were not allowed to play card games on Sundays, or on any other day for money. We never touched alcohol or swore. My father, who worked conventionally enough as an accountant in the city of London, shared with my mother what for those days were fairly progressive views of an idealistic character. They both indulged in Fabian theories derived from George Bernard Shaw and his associates, and were members of literary societies and discussion groups concerned with the exchange of ideas. The influence of Ruskin and William Morris was a strong element in their mental make-up.

When my father caught me at the age of sixteen or so smoking secretly, he was grieved rather than angry. He used to smack us with his hand on our naked buttocks by way of punishment. I can't remember what we were punished for—petty disobediences, perhaps, or—as on one occasion with me—being caught making water in the front garden in a tall clump of golden rod. I bitterly resented the smacking, which was sharp and painful and had no lasting physical effect. My father smacked on principle, and with a certain proportion of the wrath of God. Without being the Victorian heavy father, he acquired the status of the traditional paterfamilias. My mother tried to intervene when he smacked me, as these punishments always caused her acute distress; and her emotional ties with me became torn and strained by the hatred between my father and me. I didn't hate him for long at a time; and indeed our relationship was so intricate that it couldn't be called either love or hate. It was both at the same time. I longed to be loved and cared for by him, but his sense of duty as a parent stood between us. His sense of duty was based on religious principles, principles which, if strictly carried out, must make any healthy relations impossible. My father and mother were allied in two things—their religious principles and their enjoyment of humour. If I give the impression that our household was a gloomy abode of misery, that is because I am writing mainly of the dark side of my life. Openly we were gay, intellectual people with many local friends, and the house always gave the impression of convivial hospitality. We didn't miss alcohol, we never had any; and we didn't want to play cards for money. We put up with chapel because we could be secretly satirical about the minister's intellectual pretensions. Our happiness was open and apparent. It was only our misery that was secret and unshared. The cause of it was the taboo on sex.

Sex was not so much unmentioned in our family as non-existent. My father, I think, had a basically saner attitude than my mother. But the fact is that to him, just as to her, sex in most of its manifestations was dirty. My mother was prurient, and sex was never far below the surface of her thoughts, but only in a repressive sense. My parents believed in the sanctity of holy matrimony, and that was where sex began and ended. They were jealous of our friendships with the opposite sex, and at heart afraid of the explosive nature of sex. My mother would never leave me alone in the house with the maid, I think because she feared I might make love to her, but ostensibly because if the maid became pregnant, she might have to lay the blame on me. This was how my mother protected herself in her belief in my utter purity. So we enjoyed no spontaneous friendships with our equals—family life was jealously guarded. My brother and sister and I were our parents' bond of union with each other, and we meant everything to them. It is well known that the basic interest of adolescents is sex, and sex for us was taboo. Our sexual curiosity was driven underground. But of course in a literary and artistic home there are plenty of outlets for sexual curiosity. I say 'our' because I assume my brother and sister reacted to our surroundings much as I did. But we never discussed sex among ourselves. It was a secret life repressed under an iron surface of puritanism.

I used to pore for hours, when my parents were out, over bound volumes of late Victorian Royal Academy pictures, finding my way unerringly to the nudes. This theoretical knowledge of the female body gave me considerable gratification, and implanted a prurient desire to see the real thing, or as much of it as possible, as soon as possible. Parental repression must have stifled very early the natural desire to see human flesh, for I remember when, even at a dames' school I attended before going to Yattonbeck, I once caught sight of a boy's naked side between his shirt and the top of his shorts, and the experience remained in my conscious memory ever afterwards. Not that I must blame my parents entirely: indeed, understanding, not blame, is what I am trying for. Children easily affect each other with precocious puritan views, especially in a respectable, socially conscious neighbourhood. Most of my life's unhappiness derives ultimately from puritanism, of which my parents were not the inventors but only the embodiment. But theirs was a latterday puritanism—they didn't frown on pleasure so long as it was healthy. Nonconformity is perhaps, after all, the more accurate word to describe the nineteenth- and early twentieth-century version of puritanism embodied in my parents.

I became a voyeur, and voyeurism is a source of unhappiness because, like masturbation, it is a substitute, a second-hand form of experience. It is a source of unhappiness because it is by definition secretive, furtive and guilty. The growing man longs to be innocent, free, open: he longs to enjoy the beauty of human flesh without feeling that he is sinning. My father and mother believed, as I have said, that the only place where this could happen was in the marriage chamber. They were genuinely embarrassed by nudity in art. My father told me when I was grown up that he found it acutely difficult, when in Rome or Paris, to join a mixed conducted tour round the classical paintings and sculptures. My mother would betray her suppressed interest in sex at the cinema by breathing heavily whenever any passion was depicted, and it was embarrassing to be with her on such occasions.

2

In writing this account of what some would call my sexual life, but what in a broader sense I would call my emotional life, my secret or inner life, I am trying to draw out one strand from a complicated pattern of experience. I might write of reading, scholarship, writing, travel, ambition, a dozen things—but the secret strand is the most important, the one that makes sense of the whole pattern. I have never known anyone who was not more interested in sex, in one manifestation or another, than in anything else, whatever social pretences he put up, whatever sublimations his interest underwent. Some would say this is a commonplace. It was not in my youth. There used to be a theory of the 'ruling passion', by which everyone was motivated: fame, money, power and so on. All these, in the obsessive sense, are manifestations of sex or substitutes for sex. I know from my own experience that an absolutely satisfying sexual relationship displaces all other passions while it lasts; that in achieving this you achieve the object of all your other aims, whether in the direction of fame, wealth, power or intellectual distinction. Sexual satisfaction is satisfaction. Nothing else is. Thus the sexual strand is the key to every existence. Hence the need I feel to trace this strand through my life.

As I use the words 'sex' and 'sexual', I am conscious of their inadequacy. The word 'sex' is used to dissociate the specifically physical thing from its emotional and spiritual connections. 'Spiritual' is a forbidden word: I would accept 'psychic', but it means the same. 'Sex' is an attempt to become clinical about something that has become loose and vague. 'Love' is a word we now shrink from defining. It is an attempt to generalise all the feelings of nearness to a parent, a child, a mistress, an animal or even a country or a food or drink. It means either nothing or everything, out of a specific context. To substitute the word 'sex' is to evade the problem of defining what we mean. It is a useful term in some ways, but like 'love' it has become too vague and general. This, I believe, is because the thing itself—love or sex—is larger than we try to make it. There are people to whom sex, in the purely biological sense, is something they can experience and enjoy. At least I suppose so. But a sexual relationship, if it is not simply to end, must evolve into an emotional one; the specifically sexual, biological relationship may very soon end or diminish, but be replaced by an emotional one which can be called love.

Sexual experiences, desires or feelings in adolescence underlie all human relations and all activities. But the direction in which the individual's aims and desires lead him may have little to do, overtly, with sexual activities. So, in trying to understand the direction in which my impulses led me, I concentrate on the specifically physical, because it is in that area of my experience that the significance seems to lie. That is not to say that other things were of no importance: on the contrary, competitive examinations, music and so on occupied more of my time and my outward attention. But underneath, the secret life was all that mattered. The outward life, what others knew of and what I consciously pursued, was the exterior manifestation of the inner life. To speak only of the outer is like thinking of a flowerbed as if it had no roots. Love, or sex—here they are the same—has at its centre the need to console oneself for the loneliness of one's condition by contact with the body or spirit of another. So I think that my need, in all my activities, has been to assuage loneliness, to be valued for myself, to find security in duality. The generalised love of a group is better than nothing, but there is no substitute for being cared about by the individual of one's choice.

I left Yattonbeck at about the age of eleven or twelve and went to a conventional prep school, Newton Lodge, in the home counties. Although I was fond of, and good at, my studies, it was the other boys I was interested in. I was not liked by the staff because I was intellectually precocious, and brains are not liked by the staff of a conventional English public school. They applauded, they gave high marks, but they disliked. I was only partly conscious of this, but my non-acceptance by the staff gave me a feeling of inferiority, which identified itself with a conviction that I was physically unattractive. For years I suffered from this feeling, which I have learnt is very common among both boys and girls who have no reason at all for thinking so. It was obvious to me that it was the attractive boys who were liked by the staff, and this turned me into an emotional voyeur, one jealous for affection and recognition. I should say that, as a young boy of about six or seven, I had been very pretty, with a mass of pure gold curls and a beaming smile for all who made a fuss of me. I was doted on by the women teachers at kindergarten. At the age of seven or so it became necessary for me to wear spectacles, and in those days this was a hideous penance and an absolute bar to being thought good-looking. Spectacles meant abnormal brainpower, inability to play games, a preference for reading and other unhealthy activities. Just as one can be a physical voyeur, one can be an emotional voyeur, spying on the relations between boys and masters or boys and other boys. I was acutely jealous of the attention paid to other, better-looking boys.

I craved affection as a hungry man craves food. I formed a friendship with a boy called Edward, the son of a Norfolk vicar. It was not markedly physical, although we held hands after lights out in the space between our beds. We were caned together for talking in the dormitory. This was the first time I had ever been caned, and I remember little about it. The caning wasn't severe.

Edward was a charming boy, lively, intelligent and humorous. He had a delicately formed face and a smooth, pale skin. I don't recollect having been physically in love with him to any serious degree; we discussed books and motor-cars, not sex. He came to see me in my rooms years afterwards at Cambridge—having seen nothing of me during our public school years—and I found him equally charming in a more mature way. He never came to see me again. Whether he didn't like my books or decided that I meant nothing to him any longer I don't know. He had the same almost girlish, shy gentleness which has always attracted me. I have an idea he was reading for the Church.

It was at Newton Lodge that the gulf between my acts and my thoughts became wider and more final. Every boy who attracted me physically became the object of compulsive fantasies. Every night I settled down in bed with one of them in my arms. This never happened in actuality, and my power of fantasy became stronger and more elaborate. I think it was the sensation of warmth derived from imagining myself in the arms of a boy I loved which made this activity so regular and so compulsive. (I can't remember whether my fantasies were enacted naked or in pyjamas.) Probably every child goes to bed each night with something in his arms, whether a real toy or a fancied lover.

My bedtime fantasies had always been a thrilling part of my life. Towards evening I would plan my special fantasy for that evening with devoted care. I longed to be in bed to begin. At a very early stage I was regularly in love with horses, whom I would allow to stand with their forelegs on my body, knowing I could trust them not to crush me. I would occasionally sacrifice my life for a horse, or later for a beloved slave. Often the fantasy would occur on a desert island, where the relationship could be private and exclusive. Self-immolation in a cannibal's stewpot, preceded by being carved up by a sharp knife, was a frequent masochistic fantasy.

All the boys at Newton Lodge were automatically ranged in my mind into two groups, separated absolutely and categorically—those I would like to have held in my arms in bed and those I would not. One boy I was greatly attracted to was a good little cricketer. I see now that his face was of the same cast as that of Ian at Yattonbeck—grey eyes, clear skin, high cheekbones. I was still only twelve, living in a highly conventional atmosphere and capable of instinctual behaviour. Without any preliminary I kissed him in a murky hole known as the 'bootroom'. He announced this with complete sangfroid at lunch. 'Y kissed me in the bootroom this morning.'

No one seemed very interested, but I was covered with shame and embarrassment. I never again made an overture of a physical kind to anyone of my own sex until I was much older. My homosexual life became wholly secret, only occasionally guessed at by my schoolfellows and known, later, to one or two selected adult friends. The concealment gnawed at me like a slow disease.

Both my spectacles and my physical cowardice kept me apart from my companions on the cricket field and in the swimming bath. Yet I longed to be good at games, and acquired an aesthetic admiration for schoolboy cricket and some cricketers which lasted until I went to Cambridge. I admired particularly a boy called Leonard, and it was my great pleasure to share a desk with him for one term. I have said that I never fell in love with anyone older than myself, but Leonard must have been at least a year older, for he soon left to go to a public school. He was for a long time the subject of my bedtime fantasies. He was kind to me, a good cricketer and a good scholar. I had for him a ready adoration as something of a hero. I heard much later that the school to which he went was notorious for homosexual practices forced on the new boys by the seniors, so I wonder how Leonard fared, for he was a very attractive boy.

Another boy I adored at Newton Lodge was a good cricketer and the school captain. He had great physical grace and beauty, a typical fair-haired young English schoolboy, and he became my dormitory captain. It was his practice, for a time, to order the younger boys out of bed and beat them on the bottom, asking them first to bend over their beds. Despite his beauty and the reverence in which I held him, I didn't look forward to my turn: I was a physical coward and I had as yet no conscious masochistic tendencies. When my turn came, the punishment was surprisingly mild. This boy did not have it in him to hurt anyone, but he enjoyed the sensation of power. He allowed us to choose between a beating with the back of a hairbrush and one with a dressing-gown cord. Everyone chose the latter because it's almost impossible to hurt anyone with a cord made of plaited wool.

Life at Newton Lodge implanted in me my lifelong obsession with flagellation. I was myself caned three times in all—first with my friend Edward for talking in the dormitory; next for swearing when I broke a shoelace when changing to go for a school walk; thirdly for being one of a whole dormitory caught talking after lights-out. After my second caning I became notorious; the Headmaster saw fit to make an announcement about it before the assembled school after lunch. His wife and daughter and the whole staff were present. He did not name me, but everyone knew who the victim was.

'This morning,' he announced portentously, 'I had to *flog* a boy—' (he spoke the terrible word with great force, but in fact the caning had been quite mild), 'to flog a boy for swearing.' He went on to preach a short homily on the evil of swearing. Yet he was a good man and a good teacher and we admired him; no one resented him, because he had no favourites. He caned with some frequency, never getting nearer to our flesh than the seat of a pair of pyjamas. The last caning I ever had was in pyjamas. The Head came thunderously into our dormitory when most of us were talking after lights-out, despite the ineffective efforts of the dormitory prefect to stop us. Challenged to own up as to who was talking, all of us except the prefect and perhaps a couple of others leapt out of bed. Not to own up was a sin against the holy ghost. There must have been eight of us who were caned that evening. We were made to kneel down beside our beds and receive four strokes each. When the Head left the room, the silence was profound. After a few minutes I said to the prefect, 'May I be excused?' 'You don't really want to be.' 'Oh,' I said artlessly, 'I do.' Everyone knew that I wanted to have a look at my naked bottom in the bathroom mirror. But I failed in my plan since I forgot to take my spectacles with me; the vision I had in the mirror was blurred and uninteresting.

The excitement caused in the school by this mass punishment was intense. As we rose next morning, the whole of another dormitory came into ours to see us strip and show off our weals. The showing of weals on the bottom is one of the keenest pleasures known to schoolboys. The sufferer becomes a hero, and the spectator is purged by pity and terror.

Towards the end of the prep school years, as I have read elsewhere, the interest in flagellation is almost universal. There were no homosexual practices, to my knowledge, during my time at Newton Lodge. Indeed, most of us had scarcely reached the age of puberty before we left. On one occasion this same dormitory prefect, a boy I liked but was not physically attracted to, exchanged a meaning glance with me when, in the Head's Latin class, the word 'fatum' simultaneously struck his and my sense of smut. Dirty words were taboo. The Head intercepted the glance and made us stay behind after the lesson. I said to myself resignedly, 'This means twelve.' But he didn't flog us, he merely gave us a forceful talk on smut. To be fair to him, he was not unkind to me, but I could see that he didn't really like me. I was one of those dangerous nuisances—a brainy boy with power to influence others, a bookish, spectacled malcontent. We had fixed bath times, and there were no locks on the doors. One day he came into the bathroom when I was naked and pretended to fiddle with a disused gas bracket. It was only much later that I realised he had in fact come in to inspect my physical development. I must have been nearly fourteen and had indeed a sprinkling of pubic hair.

In the big schoolroom there were high sash windows, raised or lowered by means of thin, hard blind cord. It was an amusement of the prefects to make smaller boys bend over the window sill and lay their heads beneath the open window in the manner of one on the execution block. Then the window was gently lowered, and the boy was whipped on the bottom with the blind cord. This wasn't very painful, except in anticipation, and no one openly resented it. One boy whom I loved, called Clifford, was caned by the Head with some force on one occasion, and I was privileged to be shown his naked bottom privately in the lavatory. I was shocked to see a huge livid purple bruise where all the strokes must have fallen on the same spot. I felt a wave of fascinated horror and compassion sweep over me. I longed to soothe the place in some way, but could only utter some exclamation of sympathy. Many years later, when Clifford and I must have been about forty, the Head's son, who had taken over the school on his father's retirement, told me that Clifford had recently returned to the school as an adult 'old boy' and asked him to give him one stroke of the cane just to remind him of school days. The Head had jocularly complied. I feel certain that an obsession with flagellation, practical or theoretical, never leaves anyone once he has acquired it at school.

The end of my time at Newton Lodge was marked by a furtive friendship with a boy named Kenneth, who didn't attract me physically. But I liked him, and he was under a cloud for bullying. He did not bully me, as we were of an age and shortly to leave to go to the same public school. Together we enjoyed the pleasures of mutual flagellation, which we performed among some laurels on the edge of the playground, using switches we had cut for the purpose. This mutual sado-masochistic pleasure is one I have never enjoyed with anyone since. Indeed I have only once, long after those days, had the exquisite pleasure of being whipped by a friend. The whippings which Kenneth and I exchanged were certainly, though we did not know it and had no other emotional interest in each other, sexual. The pleasure which he gave me undoubtedly made me fond of him, but I never imagined myself in bed with him.

A conventional English boarding school is, or was, run on the principle that everything boys are most interested in should be suppressed. Of course we were interested in games, to a lesser extent in work, and in other officially encouraged activities. We never discussed our secret physical lives, and there was very little dirty talk. But no official encouragement was needed to foster an intense, compelling interest in flagellation—the prep school manifestation of sex. Beatings were given, but not discussed; weals were viewed with little comment by individuals or small groups. I don't think the Head derived conscious sexual satisfaction from caning; but undoubtedly his canings fostered an intense interest in the practice. I wonder what he would have done had he known that it was practised in secret by those he caned. Thus the bond that united us all was a secret one. It gave colour and excitement to a way of life basically boring and unnatural, but it increased our isolation. I suspect that most boys, like me, enjoyed their private fantasies, unaware that everyone else was doing the same.

3

I have described myself in boyhood as a prig. I adopted this persona in tribute to my mother, who believed that I must be gentlemanly in behaviour, pure in thought, word and deed. It was of course an impossible ideal, based on chapel-going criteria of conduct and attitude. I left Newton Lodge at the age of fourteen a convinced prig, an idealist. My inner life was buried safely inside me, my outer life was of hypocritical conformity to middle-class standards of respectability and moral uprightness. I was extremely ambitious, living always in the future—a fantasy life in which I should play some important part as artist, man of action and statesman : someone of power and influence. I was convinced of my own excellence, that I was unique and destined for something special. There were thus many internal compensations for my feeling of isolation from my fellows. I stood apart. I alone *knew* more than they did. I was in every way superior, yet longing to be accepted by them. This longing for influence took the form of a quick wit. I was expected to amuse and entertain. In this way I was able to compensate for what I felt to be my physical inadequacy and retain my sense of power, while having a secret, voyeuristic desire to enter into the ordinary lives of my schoolfellows.

I got a scholarship to my public school and became very soon the uncrowned head of the intellectual life of the school. Intellectual life, however, though it gave me much satisfaction, was not what I craved. I longed for emotional life, for friendship. I imagine that the history of many boys' school lives is the history of their friendships or their desire for friendship. The opportunities at Pryde, a progressive and fairly permissive school, were enormous. We had companions in class, companions in the 'House'—that is, the dormitories—and companions in the school generally, through its numerous societies. My closest friend was my study companion, Oliver, with whom I was very close. Yet I had little physical interest in him, attractive though he was. There is a kind of non-sexual fondness between boys deprived of feminine companionship which can be very rewarding, even if there is no question of homosexuality. Oliver in any case developed chronic acne early on which, so to speak, kept me at a distance. He had great trouble with his complexion, and I sympathised. We remained close friends throughout our school career. He told me that at his prep school the Headmaster's wife had ruled the school, and that she did so with a bundle of twigs, applied with force to the small boys' naked bottoms. She was evidently a vicious woman with a strong personality.

I sought everywhere for friendship with boys I could admire physically. In my dormitory there was a boy of extreme physical beauty, for whom I lusted throughout my school life. His face was long and high-cheeked, his skin perfect, his mouth full, his nose gracefully tip-tilted. His body was slender, perfectly formed, loosely knit; his hair dark and somewhat drooping. He had a bewitching smile and a puckish sense of humour. He was, to many admirers, essentially a girl. His body remained hairless and he did not attain puberty till a late age, nearly sixteen I think. I remember hearing him emerge from what had evidently been an intimate conference with his study companions, saying, 'So now I'm a *pubes*'. His companions hushed him, as the subject was taboo, but the discovery, I imagine, gave him relief and satisfaction. His body was beautiful, and I remember engaging him in a mock wrestling match on his bed one evening. Drawing down his pyjama trousers, I beat his naked bottom with my hand in a loving playful way. He was in every way a boy of normal attachments, with no visible trace of homosexuality. He was the sort who would probably become a comfortable country solicitor. I loved him dearly. He had the open, obvious beauty that comes into the world to give pleasure of a free and innocent kind to many. He was never the subject of scandal, though I noticed that boys with hidden homosexual tendencies sought his company, as I did.

Another boy in my dormitory was a coarse, badly spoken, good-natured extrovert who soon took on his neighbour Ivan as what he called his 'slave'. Ivan was a red-haired boy with a regular, handsome face and a skin of extreme smoothness and whiteness. I secretly lusted for him, but never came very near.

Two boys in the dormitory became the butts of our sadistic instincts. One was stupid, the other grossly fat. We stripped them and beat them with wet towels. I joined in this sport with an intense feeling of guilt, because I was fond of one of them, not for his fat pink body, but for his gentleness and kindness. I bullied him very little, and we became friends and, later, smoking companions in the public lavatory in the nearby town. His fatness, glandular in origin, caused him great unhappiness, and this unhappiness made him kind and sensitive. The fact is, I think, that physical beauty, the quality that gets a boy or a girl admirers, is often a fatal gift; it may make the possessor insensitive and oblige him or her to develop a hardness of character sufficient to repel unwanted attention. It would have been deeply satisfying to have had an emotional relationship with a boy such as my fat friend, but the necessary initial physical attraction was simply not there.

The passion, the craving, the greed for physical beauty, by which I was surrounded at Pryde, became a daylong, almost a nightlong obsession. It was never gratified except in fantasy. But every day I would seek out the opportunity to be near some boy who aroused my lust. I habitually made the adolescent mistake of associating physical beauty with mental or moral distinction. I invested my love-objects with qualities of nature and intellect with which most of them were certainly not endowed. Yet I believe that the beautiful are different from the rest of us, in that the admiration and desire they attract are radiated back from them, and people are happy in their presence. Life at Pryde would perhaps have been more satisfying if the homosexuality I felt to be in the air had been more openly acknowledged. It never was. In those days at any rate there was an air of innocence about the place that would have made any overt atmosphere of homosexuality wholly unwelcome. I remember only one scandal in my time—the alleged association of a very coarse, brutal type of boy in my house with a gentle, feminine, rather stupid creature. They were reported to go off into the woods together for the pursuit of unnatural practices. But no one knew the details, and no one enquired closely. The masters, all of whom were unmarried, followed the Headmaster's example in being platonically homosexual; not all of them, of course, but a number. Celibacy was commoner in those days than now, and it was often followed by a rather belated marriage.

A great many boys attracted me, and I sought their presence and was generally liked by them because I think they never suspected my real interest. I can see one of them now, a boy with fair hair and intense dark eyes whom I admired, but with whom I had nothing in common; another, who had a reputation for being somewhat feminine—indeed he was nicknamed Cleopatra and was the object of attention for a number of us. I was once accused of gazing with unusual interest at Cleopatra while watching a football match. 'Half the house saw you,' I was told. Without hesitation I replied: 'It's easy to see which half' and there was no further comment.

I wish I knew now how much suppressed homosexuality was hidden under the outwardly public school conventionality of Pryde. I certainly was never seriously suspected of such tendencies. I was tortured by another matter which was more or less taboo—masturbation. I marvel even now at the obsessive quality of this activity. To the habitual masturbator masturbation *is* his life, or a great part of it. He longs to be free of it. If a day perhaps a week passes without indulgence, he feels a new man; but he knows he is in the grip of it and will not long be free. He says, 'Wait—not until Friday, not for another week.' He dares himself not to masturbate, and the stronger his resolve, the greater his humiliation and shame when he falls. The worst years are perhaps between fifteen and eighteen. For years I tortured myself, day and night, trying to escape from this incubus, but there was no escape.

When lights were out and I was warm in bed, my fantasy would play on the body of someone I admired, my penis would stir and stand up; I would resist; then, untying my pyjama trousers, I would lie on my back, give myself up to pure sensation and achieve a climax of agonised ecstasy. Sometimes I masturbated by sheer compulsion, sometimes deliberately, preparing myself for pleasure by a prolonged fantasy. At other times I had no physiological compulsion but merely did it for the sensation, too soon after the last time to be able to achieve any spontaneity: accordingly I would flay an artificial erection with savage self-loathing.

On one occasion a dormitory prefect said sarcastically, 'Enjoying yourself, Y?' but I took no notice. No one could be sure what went on under the bedclothes. I took no precautions to prevent the sperm from coagulating on my sheets and pyjamas, and so noticeable did this become that the house matron commented on it. She was as nervous as I felt, and I brushed her comment aside with a lie. My housemaster, a retired army man and a bachelor, lectured us all individually on sex, about which he knew little. 'Do you ever feel tempted to abuse yourself?' he asked. I said I did not. 'If I am,' he told me, 'I pray.' I respected him for this. I remember asking him if it did any harm. He answered, 'No, I suppose not, but it weakens the will.' It does more than this: it confirms in the masturbator the habit of withdrawal from life. It is a substitute, and the substitute may become more acceptable than the reality. When I was about eighteen I swore I would give up masturbation at the age of twenty. I have never given it up.

Sometimes I masturbated twice or three times a day for several days on end. Once I masturbated in a lesson of higher mathematics. I masturbated in the bath, in the lavatory, in public lavatories, in my study on a warm afternoon. There seemed to be no limit to the imprisoned potency which longed to be released. It would be hypocritical to deny that it gave me my most intense pleasure; but it was a pleasure dissociated from normal relationships. It emphasised my loneliness, isolation and despair. My love relations with boys were idealistic, sentimental. I pictured their bodies to myself, but I never imagined myself at all interested in their genitals; I never contemplated sodomy. In my fantasy, indeed, they scarcely had genitals. I thought of myself simply as settling down in bed with them, my arms around them, caressing their backs, their thighs, their buttocks, kissing them and stroking their hair.

There was a young boy in another house whom it gave me intense pleasure to see occasionally and exchange words with, though we had little in common. He was, I think, the object of the secret lust of his house captain, a boy much older than he. He was a boy of great beauty—prettily built, with a long, high-cheeked, dark-eyed face I loved, and it was inevitable that I should desire him. One evening I met him on the way to post some letters. 'Have you any stamps?' he asked. I gave him the two stamps he wanted, and he put his hand in his pocket for the money to pay me with. 'I don't want any money, Jones,' I said. 'I'd rather give you them.' He was genuinely surprised and touched. 'Oh thanks,' he said 'You're —you're the nicest chap I've met this evening.' I hugged the thought, and Jones, in bed that night.

Anyone reading these pages might think either that my homosexuality was imaginary or that I was not very highly sexed, except perhaps in brief phases. I can't analyse myself, I can only record. One knows everything about oneself, but one doesn't know oneself. Certainly I can see that what attracted me in boys were the feminine qualities—prettiness, grace, smoothness, gentleness, softness of speech. My overruling desire was to hug and caress them in secret. It was the same with girls, at least until my later school days. I was looking for a love-object, a friend who should be wholly mine and with whom I could have relations of physical intimacy. I never found such an object, and no one I desired was given any hint that I felt for him even a romantic passion, yet such were the almost exclusive objects of my thoughts.

Another aspect of my situation was its irrationality, its

illogicality. I never proposed to do anything active to gratify my desire. I had, perhaps, a narcissistic conviction that love would come to me, that it would be a spontaneous occurrence between the object and myself. I never even touched another boy, much less spoke out my feelings. This is not, now I think of it, strictly true. There was a charming boy in another house who attracted me in a remote kind of way, and one day the whole school was grouped for one of those mammoth, long photographs which all schools go in for. I found myself immediately behind this boy, and the photograph, to my embarrassment, recorded that my hand rested on his shoulder. No mention was ever made of this, but some boys must have commented. The whole thing was under such a taboo that we all behaved as if it did not exist. There must have been many in my situation, but very few of the boys or men I have ever been attracted to had any homosexual tendencies. It seemed as if any practical realisation of my fantasies was out of reach of the real world, and I accepted this with resignation. Yet the fantasies were compelling and unremitting. When I went to bed and chose a love-object to embrace, the warmth of my body and my thoughts would inevitably generate the urge to masturbate. Before me was the prospect of nothing but waste and sterile emotionalism. I invented of course a character for each love-object which must have been wholly alien to his real nature.

Adrian was an attractive, petite boy with the same grey eyes, clear skin and regular, round features that had attracted me to the boy I had kissed in the bootroom at Yattonbeck. He had no particular intellectual distinction, but we liked one another and would go for walks. His grace of movement and gentle speech were irresistible. We indulged in—or rather I pressed upon him—as a substitute for sex a lot of soulful talk, to which he listened with respect. 'You're so much *higher* than I am,' he sighed. I heard this with gratification mixed with regret, for it distanced him from me. He had not, I am convinced, much, if any homosexuality. One day he produced a book containing reproductions of pictures by Watts. Turning to one of Faith leading Love over the rocks (or something like that), in which a naked winged angel leads a naked young woman over a stony path, he said: 'I don't think that body's very beautiful, do you?' He indicated the female figure, whose angular buttock did indeed strike me as unattractive. I think now of the paths along which I might have led this conversation had I been more experienced and less of a moral prig. But I had, I see it now, the expectation that love would come to me without effort; and I think the basis of this was a sense of pride: to enjoy love one must be prepared for the humiliation of rejection. There is also, of course, the risk of exposure and gossip. I always had a morbid fear of being talked about, even with approval.

My grand passion at Pryde lasted for my final three years. It was for a boy of my own age in another house. He was gentle, beautifully spoken, kind, sensitive and not very intelligent. He was an excellent player of cricket and rugger, at which game he achieved some international fame. But he had none of the obvious character of an athlete. He was modest, unexhibitionistic, what would perhaps have been called a 'sound' rather than a brilliant performer. His face was not, compared with some that attracted me, markedly beautiful: his skin was clear and fair, with a very slightly sallow look; his eyes were slightly compressed into slits, as if by the height of his cheekbones; his face was oval, his hair slightly curled and of a medium brown colour. He had a sort of classic beauty almost beyond possession, but his appearance was not breath-taking. Everybody liked him. To be with him was relaxing; his presence had a calming effect.

I found myself in love with him—or rather, I found him suddenly in complete possession of my thoughts and fantasies. I longed to be near him, to talk to him. I would try to exchange a few words with him in passing as often as I could, and a day in which I didn't contrive to speak to him was marked down as a black day in my life. There is a deep humility in romantic love which asks for little, and is satisfied with, or at least thankful for, little.

We would talk together, and I think he was grateful for the interest of one of the most intellectual scholars in the school. He was very much aware of his own lack of intellect, and his one desire was to get into Oxford. He never succeeded in passing the school Certificate exam, which would have enabled him to sit for Oxford. I spent many exquisite half-hours coaching him in the Shakespeare paper, but to no avail. I adored Brian and would cheerfully have died for him. We discussed poetry, of which he remembered some that he had read. It was the day of Rupert Brooke. I learnt that he was the only son of a widowed mother without a lot of money, and this gave him added glamour and excited my compassion.

The affair, if it can be called that, died out when I left school, and I never saw him again, though we exchanged a few letters. Its climax, so far as I was concerned, was when I saw, for the first and last time, Brian's naked body. His house occupied changing rooms next to ours. They were separated from ours by the wire netting cages in which we kept our sports gear. It was very easy to look through them at our neighbours as they stripped, bathed and dressed again after a game or a cross-country run. It was the ideal situation for voyerism. Indeed, it was not necessary to look through the wire netting, as one's own house was also stripping and having shower baths around one. You were expected to behave as if there were no naked boys about you; you were thought to be wholly uninterested in the male body. I hardly believe that any of us were indifferent. Surely any naked body is exciting—even if it excites only disgust by its grossness or malformation. We were, on the whole, a good-looking lot of boys. Indeed, I suspect that the Headmaster, who interviewed all applicants, never turned down an Adonis, however simple-minded. He knew he needed scholars too; hence the success of such bespectacled, prematurely bearded creatures as I. I have never since had the opportunity to see so many young, naked male bodies as I had then, and the sight gave me infinite pleasure. The simile of the Greek god is outworn, but conveys the right impression. Just as I divided my clothed schoolfellows, judging by their faces, into those I would have liked to kiss and those I would not, so I judged them when stripped by their beauty of form and skin, and divided them into those who aroused my lust and those who did not. A taut, slender, graceful body with a smooth belly, well-formed buttocks, cleanly moulded shoulders, straight, rounded thighs tapering to slim ankles—in short a body approximating to the classic beauty of Michelangelo's David—this was a source of inner satisfaction that nothing else has ever given me. It filled me with a profound melancholy because it seemed, in the context of English public school life, unaware of its own beauty, innocent, chaste and remote. It seems to me almost tragic that the English have had their natural sensuality stifled by chill, Calvinistic Puritanism, and that they are forced to realise it only in fantasy and furtiveness. If only there could have been open admiration of a boy whose radiant beauty anyone, even a philistine, must have been aware of, if only it had been possible to lay one's hands on his naked shoulders, or stroke his belly and say, 'My god, how beautiful you are! Aren't you proud of such a body?'—how much spontaneous happiness would have been generated. As it was, custom dictated that we looked at a roomful of steaming, naked, healthy young bodies as if they were so many sandbags. The nearest anyone came to expressing admiration or interest was squirting cold water over a friend or affectionately slapping his wet bottom with a towel.

To see my friend Brian naked through the wire-netting was an exquisite agony. It happened only once, after a cross-country run. He was as beautiful as I had imagined he would be—straight, slender but sturdy, an athlete but without the exaggerated bulges of a wrestler or a weight-lifter. He didn't see me. I longed to rush round and embrace him, fall down and put my arms round his waist in silent admiration. As it was, I had to behave as if he didn't exist, as if I had no eyes.

Until I was middle-aged I often wondered if I was ever the object of a passively homosexual interest. I don't think I was, not at any rate since the relationship with Ian at the age of ten. There is perhaps one exception, which I shall come to shortly. I knew a boy at Pryde who did not attract me at all, but as he lived within a mile of my home and shared my literary interests, I saw him from time to time. I never suspected homosexual tendencies in him. He showed no sign of them while he was at school, and his name was never mentioned in this context. From this I infer that there were many other passive homosexuals or bisexuals at school; but I did not imagine this at the time. I believed that I alone suffered from this guilty, or at least shameful tendency. The subject was taboo, and that was that. We knew of course of tendencies to romantic friendship and mutual attraction between boys, but we were not especially interested in the subject; or if we were, we hid it. It must also be remembered that I was still a prig, outwardly pure and puritanical. I felt therefore that my tendency was something to be concealed, though privately I was not in the least ashamed of it. The spontaneous inner joy I experienced through the physical attractiveness of many boys was too great for me to feel any genuine private guilt or even shame. It turned out that after he left school this boy served a prison sentence for what the courts call 'interfering' with a small boy or boys. I never heard the details, and I didn't know of this until long afterwards. The family left the neighbourhood and I forgot them. It was, I think, sad that society had to condemn a boy so sensitive and intelligent for following his natural instincts. He was not a rough type. On the contrary, with a certain prettiness which did not appeal to me, he was more like the object of a homosexual attachment than the active partner. I cannot condemn homosexuals as such—indeed I have never done so—but I still cannot condone the corruption of the young, those unable to choose for themselves. It is the desire of the vast majority of men to enjoy heterosexual relations, and to predispose a minor exclusively to the other kind of relation must be wrong. I feel certain that, although far more men than is generally thought have at least a small proportion of positive homosexuality in their make-up, the young must, so to speak, have the benefit of the doubt. Although I think homosexual or partly homosexual friendships can be of great comfort and benefit to individuals, it is right to regard it as a form of corruption actively to encourage such a tendency in a boy. The law is right to condemn this.

There was a boy at Pryde called Bernard Hough, whom I liked but found quite unattractive physically. His features were irregular, his colouring and complexion not of the kind that attracted me. He spoke with a certain affectation, and this was a bar to my whole-hearted acceptance of him; for my puritanism also contained an element of scorn for anything affected, anything not plain and direct. But Bernard was sensitive and intelligent, and I encouraged him to come to my study and talk. He clearly enjoyed doing this. I was older, and he evidently looked up to me. For all I knew, he cherished unspoken hero-worship. I have, actually, always been embarrassed by expressions of approval from people who do not attract me, unless I respect them as my equals or superiors in mental qualities. I would prefer the approval of a fool, naturally, to his disapproval, but neither affects me much, one way or another. But Bernard was no fool, and I was touched and flattered, even though faintly embarrassed, when he came back from the town one day with a present that could only be some kind of love-gift. It was a sumptuous edition of the poems of Longfellow in crushed black leather. Some might say that my dislike of the poems of Longfellow stems from my rejection of Bernard, but this is not so. I tried to like them. I think Bernard wanted friendship, being perhaps as hungry as I for it; he had not many friends at Pryde.

We had a young and vigorous Head at Pryde, and a young and keen staff. 'Sex' life, therefore, was not lurid at that time, as in accounts of some other public schools at certain periods. So far as I knew, few boys had had any heterosexual relations, though these were the subject of muttered conversations in studies and dormitories. I fancy that my puritan attitude towards sex-talk, swearing and bawdy made my fellows keep quiet in my presence, perhaps out of mistaken respect for my prejudices; so that I probably never knew what went on. Nothing much went on, I think, because scandal gets about, and I had an ear for scandal. The policy of the school was in most respects highly enlightened, and there were always numerous activities for the canalisation or sublimation of excessive energy. A general aura of passive 'Greek' romantic homosexuality was diffused, having as its source the Head himself. He was a bachelor and enjoyed open, harmless friendships with a few boys whom he evidently favoured. But his palpable, unspoken preferences made me jealous. I was not, as I have said, attractive to members of my own sex, and this increased my isolation and despair.

The Head was in fact alarmed at any prospect of carnal love. There was an outbreak, shortly after I left, of such relations in one particular house. A number of boys were found in each others' beds enjoying what could justly be called a romantic proximity. There were several expulsions, and among them was a very beautiful boy whose dazzling blond hair and classic features, together with his athleticism, made him the object of secret homosexual passion. At least one member of the staff hardly made a secret of his admiration, and the boy was taken on swimming expeditions to remote places and photographed in the nude, usually from behind, sitting on the ground. So innocent was this behaviour that some of the photographs were shown openly, and aroused little comment. In the more permissive atmosphere of today this could hardly happen. The master was actually bisexual and cured himself of deviation by getting married.

The boy, Vernon, who was younger than I and whom I scarcely got to know at Pryde, but knew better afterwards, had a long series of unsatisfactory marriages from early manhood to middle age with women who threw themselves at him. Perhaps he suffered from suppressed homosexuality, but he later assured me that he had no streak of it in him. He and I, I remember, went for a car drive one warm summer evening, found a secluded place on the slope of a meadow and undressed. There we lay, naked, until the sun began to sink. I made no advances to him, content to admire the beauty of his athletic, naked body. No, I was not content—I longed to caress his sun-tanned skin, but I knew I was not permitted to. Moreover, I was pleased myself to be naked, because my body, unlike my face, was well-made and well-proportioned.

I was not ashamed of it, as I was of my face. My own body gave me for many years a narcissistic pleasure, and I was proud of its health, grace and vigour. I hated clothes and strongly approved of the movement then beginning for sunbathing which had spread from Germany. *Nacktkultur*, as it was called, was part of the youth movement which appealed to me. It seemed to me a daring advance in the direction of lifting those veils of Victorian prudery which had made the most beautiful object in nature something to be ashamed of. The revolution that was beginning then has so long ago succeeded that a young person of today can hardly imagine the sense of emancipation felt in the thirties.

On his side the friendship with Vernon was intellectual. (If as many people had warmed their hands on my flesh as have warmed their minds on my intellect, life would have been very different.) We were never wholly out of touch, though for years we did not meet. We occasionally corresponded. I saw him last when I was over fifty and he was in his late forties, and so attractive was he still that I made tentative love to him, which he respected with a gentle kindness. I reminded him of the time when we had stripped together, and he told me he had completely forgotten it. He was always a target for the attentions of oversexed women, and he always found them irresistible. What sexual satisfaction any of them achieved I have never discovered. It is now the fashion to say that Don Juans are homosexuals in disguise or even impotent, but I doubt if Vernon was either. He, after all, unlike Don Juan, was not the hunter but the hunted.

The Head, an enlightened traditionalist, firmly believed in the use of the cane, which was strictly regulated. A caning by him was the supreme punishment short of expulsion; housemasters were allowed to cane, as were prefects—but no one else. The Head's canings were reputed to be very severe, and they were dreaded, but I never saw nor heard direct evidence of them. I was never caned at Pryde myself. None of the housemasters was reputed to enjoy caning for its own sake. One alone was conspicuous for the frequency and savagery of his canings. He was dreaded by his house, and everyone was sorry for those in it. Yet his ferocity stemmed, I think, not from any form of perversion but from a simple ambition to make his house the best disciplined in the school. He was quite humourless and a fervent admirer of Frederick the Great. But he had many good qualities, and I was always grateful for his kindness to me and his showing me especial favour in several ways. He gave me occasional presents in the form of books. Perhaps he was an inactive homosexual, in love with me: if so, he kept it very dark. He later married and left, to become head of another school.

Prefects' beatings were another matter. I certainly heard discussion among our house prefects, with whom I was on excellent terms, as to technique in using the cane to best effect. But I think caning was used, not so much as an outlet for frustrated sexual appetite as for the gratification of a growing sense of power common among adolescents verging on manhood.

No one was caned when I was at Pryde otherwise than decorously, with trousers on. I don't recall that anyone was even caned in pyjamas. The Head's ideas were all pervasive. The caning code emanated from him and was treated, at any rate outwardly, by the masters as an unpleasant necessity, to keep order. I was on one occasion so rude to a weak master that my housemaster, in sheer spontaneous disgust, threatened to cane me, senior though I was. He would undoubtedly have been right to do so, though I froze with terror at the threat. It passed off, and was certainly effective in improving my culpable behaviour towards this master. The Head also, as I have said, set the tone of idealistic, platonic, diffused homosexuality—christian names, informal relations between masters and boys, picking of innocent favourites by masters among the younger and prettier boys. All had their favourites—or most at any rate, and these boys had a sort of Ganymede relationship to their admirers, doing little services for them in exchange for minor privileges. In view of the Head's personality and views as I knew them, it was a surprise to me to hear from a young man who had been at Pryde fifteen years or so after I had left that this boy had earned for himself, by some piece of open rebellion, a Headmaster's caning. The Head offered him the choice between twelve strokes in his trousers or nine on the naked buttocks. He must then have been a good-looking boy: he was still personable when I met him a dozen or more years later. The boy chose the smaller number of strokes. The Head administered the strokes and then gave the boy a glass of sherry!

4

I don't know if the asexuality of my family life as a boy, if I can call it that, ever struck my parents as unusual. There were girls among the children of their friends, and there were boys. We were all simply young people. From the age of fifteen it would be natural that any interest I showed in a girl was potentially sexual, and it seems to me, on looking back, that my mother was afraid of sex. I don't know why. It was, after all, the process by which she had become the mother of three children who were the aim and object of her existence. Anything that might come up in talk, in reading or on the screen which had to do with the physiological side of sex was simply avoided—at any rate so far as relations outside marriage were concerned. As for relations inside marriage, well, they were taken for granted as in a sense the purpose of marriage, and therefore there was no need to be aware of them. I think my parents regarded, or thought they had to regard, sex as sin. It was also something to be profoundly afraid of. There was another motive too: possessiveness. Sex is the avenue by which a child achieves independence from its parents, and parents may bitterly resent its appearance in their children.

And yet, illogically, my mother wanted us to 'mix' with other children. We had tennis parties, boating parties, picnics and later, dances. We were encouraged to enjoy as much contact as possible with boys and girls of our own age in a social setting. Outside the social setting, usually accompanied by adults, we had no contact.

In one sense I made no distinction, so far as my affections were concerned, between boys and girls—they were warm, attractive young people with whom I craved intimacy. I never doubted that permanent and lasting relations would be achieved with the opposite sex, leading to marriage, home and children. After I left my prep school and when I had attained the age of puberty, girls naturally became attractive; boys less so, except when I was at boarding school, away from home. I am assured by boys who went only to day schools and lived at home that homosexual tendencies are just as easily nourished by a grammar as by a public school. Yet I think the deprivation of female company of one's own age must do much to sharpen the desire for emotional fulfilment from one's own sex. In my case I am sure this was so, for most of the boys to whom I was attracted had markedly feminine traits both in appearance and personality: the ostentatiously virile and hairy did not attract me.

I could never show any special interest in a particular girl without attracting my mother's notice, and I'm sure there was an element of possessive jealousy in her attitude. I longed to fondle and caress pretty girls, but it was not possible to do this in company, and I was seldom alone. Accordingly, the presence of a girl who aroused my desire was a torture. She became a symbol of the unattainable, the mysterious, the never-to-be-possessed. My encounters with girls were furtive and inexpressive: I imagined I fell in love with many whom I knew and saw at parties, dances and other social occasions. They became the subject of my fantasies at night. I undressed them as a matter of course, hating myself with a puritanical contempt even as I did so. I wasn't interested in their genitals, of whose appearance I had no very clear notion, despite my interest in statuary and the nude in painting. I was interested almost exclusively in their breasts, and now that I have no compelling interest in women's breasts, I find it hard to imagine the state of tortured prurience into which these swellings under the blouse or the dance dress threw me. I idealised girls of course; I imagined that a girl's sweetness and kindness of nature, her love for me, if only it could ever be revealed, were in exact proportion to her physical attractions.

I believe that my desire for the girls of my acquaintance was in exact proportion to that of all the other boys of my age and circle. Those universally acknowledged as the prettiest were the prettiest to me. I know now that I was not physically unattractive to girls, but I was obsessed with the conviction that I was. This made me painfully diffident. It never occurred to me to make love to a girl. The reasons for this were several: firstly, she might reject me, and that would be a mortification to my vanity that I could not bear. Secondly, she might accept me, and that might be worse, since I should not know what to do about it. I could not go to bed with her or marry her, and I had no thought of a long and youthful engagement. Love would come by itself; to go out and get it by means of flirtation, trickery or any sort of stratagem was utterly unworthy of the standards I had set myself. Love was simply something that happened, as in an Arthurian romance, and when it happened it would be all-consuming; nothing less would do. I was very serious, very priggish. I needed an older friend and confidant, and I never had one until I was an undergraduate. I was lonely to the point of solipsism. What an adolescent boy needs is a friendship with a girl to whom he can talk, in whom he can confide, with no special demands of sex or lust. I never had such a friend. My mother guarded me from it. My sister had a friend with whom I would have gone out to the theatre or for a walk: I liked her, but was not especially attracted to her. When it became known that I contemplated taking her out, my mother said, 'I suppose you know that there is insanity in the family?' I never took the girl out, or was left in her company alone.

It was clear that any girl whom I went out with would have to have my mother's tacit approval. Moreover, the prospective relationship, however remote, would always be hinted at, and I could never expose myself to open scrutiny by my mother.

But nature intervenes. There was an exceedingly pretty little girl of our acquaintance for whom I secretly lusted. She was vivacious and flirtatious; she had been to a local day school and was not inhibited by the conventions of propriety which afflicted girls who went to private schools. I cannot say that I was in love with Betty, but she attracted me, as she wanted to. Her mother had a small car with a dickey seat. Once after my mother and I had been to tennis with them, and she had brought us home afterwards in order to collect some vegetables we had promised, I sat next to Betty in the dickey seat, a rug over our two laps. I found myself pressed against her thigh. I burned to take her hand and caress her: I was expected to but I hadn't the courage to do it. We got out and went into the garden to gather vegetables. As we bent over the basket into which we were putting brussel sprouts, Betty said to me, smiling very prettily and reproaching me with roguish playfulness, 'Some people miss all their opportunities.' This remark was shattering. I was flattered but mortified. She had actually wanted me to caress her! I said nothing, but in passionate remorse crushed my hand down upon hers as we packed the sprouts into the basket. It was of course too late, and no opportunity reoccurred to press my advantage. This kind of frustration seemed to be the keynote of all my relationships. I never had those so-called 'harmless flirtations' which are an adolescent's best introduction to sex, I took it all too seriously.

This was in fact the first time I had touched a girl—except of course for the kind of chaste contact afforded by a conventional dance in which two hands are held, the girl's left hand on the boy's shoulder, and the boy's right hand round the girl's waist as firmly as he dares. Since dancing took place in the presence of our elders, it was always with the greatest propriety. All the more could it be a torture. The girls to whom I was not attracted I danced with from a sense of duty; yet there was usually one, or perhaps two, with whom I thought myself in love. So most of the time I spent scheming as to how often I dared ask her to dance. The girls of our circle were usually as formal and proper as myself; there must have been something in me which prevented familiarity. Yet there were one or two girls with that forwardness which is such a joy to the shy boy. There was Jean, who made it obvious that the harder I grasped her, the better she liked it. There was a way of ending a foxtrot in the twenties which consisted in holding your partner very tight and whirling her round to the closing strains of the music. On such occasions Jean would press her stomach hard against mine, and the sexual satisfaction this gave to both of us was very consoling. 'I love it when you do that,' she would breathe. (This kind of girl was known among the boys as a 'belly-plasterer'.)

I think that my very diffidence made me attractive to some girls. They must have regarded my reserve, my apparent indifference, as a challenge. I have often looked back on what I regard as lost opportunities, but perhaps they were not really opportunities at all. There was one slim, beautiful athlete whom I admired with a doglike devotion, contriving to partner her at tennis as often as possible, and on such occasions playing even worse than ever. How I expected our relationship to develop, since I never dared say anything personal, I don't know, but she must have been aware of my admiration. We had tennis parties that lasted all day and were followed by supper and dancing to the gramophone. One day I was standing idly by myself on the verandah when she strolled by, racquet in hand. I happened to be whistling a tune then popular—'I ain't nobody's darling'. 'That's hard luck,' she said provocatively. I said nothing; I'm not sure that I even saw what she was getting at till afterwards. What a load of remorse in later years can one lay upon oneself by one casual act of impercipience, stupidity or cowardice. But to have made her the right answer I should have had to be a different person.

My interest in heterosexuality during my school days was largely theoretical, private and voyeuristic, like my interest in homosexuality, though with added unreality. After all, I had seen naked boys but not naked girls. The bathing costumes of those days were not very revealing, and so a furtive interest in pictures was compulsive, and any photographic representation, however 'artistic', of a naked female body aroused my keenest interest. I remember an occasion when I got hold of a number of *The Studio*, a blameless artistic magazine, and took it into a sixth form period in the library. It contained more than the usual number of nudes, which gave me great pleasure. I looked through it, while waiting for the master to arrive, with a friend sitting beside me. As we turned the pages we enjoyed the pictures of naked women, sexless as the artists' intentions were. They were not photographs but paintings and drawings. Still, they gave us pleasure. A prefect saw what we were doing and reported us to the Headmaster. He called me up, told me that the prefect had reported me and I was told to bring the magazine. The Head went through it with me, saying that this or that was harmless; whereas of course *this*—indicating a picture in which a woman's pubic hair was shown—was rather more doubtful in its effect. The Head was a man of the world and explained that I shouldn't look at *The Studio* in the presence of that particular prefect, who he said would 'go off like a fountain' if exposed to such revelations. I considered the extreme sexuality of the prefect, as implied by the Head, with some respect and awe. He had, in fact, I think, homosexual tendencies, and perhaps the depiction of the naked female body upset him. I bore him no resentment; indeed, he was always kind to me and I liked him. He was the son of a soldier, whom he addressed as 'Sir'—a sad case.

Pictures, and especially photographs, of naked bodies always fascinated me, as they do everyone else. They are, in the life of most English boys, a source of secret delight and gloating. Photos of naked men were not easy to come by, but photos of women appeared in magazines such as *Lilliput*, and I made a small collection of these, which I used to bring out, one at a time, and take to the lavatory. Once there, I used to masturbate, using the women in the photo as a fantasy sex-object. (This must be so common as to be hardly worth recording.) I once stole a book of artistic child-studies—photos of naked girls and boys in natural surroundings. It was, I think, called *Pan's Garden*, and it was several years before I grew tired of it and burnt it. I derived intense pleasure from it, making my personal selection among the children photographed. Those who were too young—mere cherubic infants—I rejected; girls with budding breasts interested me, as did boys old enough to be called boys and not children. Those with muscular legs and smooth, taut buttocks attracted me most, and it was with one or other of these that I curled up in bed at night and dropped off to sleep.

I have often wondered what life would be like without these intense, passionate and compulsive fantasies. I can imagine a kind of madness developing out of deprivation; and I feel certain that those wretched men who get into court for sexual attacks on children and young women are people lacking in imagination, without the power of rich fantasising to relieve their desire for warm human flesh.

Perhaps also they are men who derive no pleasure from masturbation. I have known one or two young men who, without being in any way undersexed, derive no satisfaction from masturbation. I envy them, for I have often regarded masturbation as the most depressing thing in my life. My housemaster's warning that masturbation weakened the will seemed to me at the time a mere formula since, if one had no will to resist, how could the will be weakened? But he was an honest man, and in a sense I think now that he was right. Even a habitual masturbator—perhaps a habitual more than an occasional one—feels the compulsion as a chain from which he struggles to free himself. Exciting as masturbation is, he knows—even a virgin knows—that it is a poor substitute, that it is sterile, unproductive, unsatisfying. So he strives to get rid of the habit and reserves his potency for what nature intended. The misery of masturbation lies in its privateness, it shuts the masturbator into himself, imprisons him in his own flesh. He knows that sex is intended to liberate him, to unite him with another, to make him outgoing. We are told that it does no harm. On a strictly physiological level this may be true, but it damages a man on the psychological level because it makes orthodox sex in some way unsatisfactory. The sexual act delights because it satisfies the desire to give pleasure to another. It is the most intimate and personal caress possible for a lover towards his lover. If the love-object is himself, the act is narcissistic. He masturbates because he is sorry for himself. He comes to pity, to love, and then to hate his own flesh.

Masturbation is the one subject which boys, outspoken and uninhibited in other ways, rarely discuss with each other. They are unwilling to admit its hold over them. This is because it gives them a sense of guilt, even of sin. Even smutty jokes about masturbation were uncommon when I was at school. I know that mutual masturbation between young boys is common, and it seems to me that this is healthier than secret masturbation. A secret shared and a guilt shared is a burden halved. I masturbated habitually and compulsively throughout my school life. I have a considerable degree of fatalism in my nature, and I believe this to be connected with the hold over me which masturbation had. If I cannot free myself from this, I reasoned, how can I ever free myself from any dictate of fate? It isn't my fault, if I'm made like this, I must act like this. I was a psychological determinist, as I still am.

I gained relief by reading, but I read sexually stimulating books only in secret. They couldn't be discussed with or shown to my parents. This is partly why it was such a relief to me to leave Pryde and go to Cambridge, where I could discuss avant-garde literature openly with my equals. One day I was reading Marcel Proust's *A l'Ombre des Jeunes Filles en Fleur* in French. My mother could understand French, but not sexual symbolism; my father was the reverse. 'In the shadow of young girls in flower,' my mother translated. 'Whatever does it mean?' 'Puberty,' said my father promptly. There was no further discussion. To the sensitive adolescent sex is indeed a shadow, though a shadow relieved by eternal hope. But hope unfulfilled is not different from despair. The deprived adolescent turns easily to despair, which is easier and more comforting than hope. Masturbation gets a hold on him because it is the act of despair. If sexual intercourse is death, as in a sense it is, masturbation is suicide. For me the ache of adolescence was only made tolerable by the almost daily comfort of thoughts of suicide. Had I had anyone to talk to, things would have been different. I felt unloved, I had no confidant, no confessor. I had no one to talk to, I kept no diary and I hadn't the creative urge to sublimate my loneliness in writing or painting. I dissipated my creative energy in dilettante amusements—playing the piano indifferently, for instance. It was all diffused sex, aimless and without direction. But I was ambitious, intellectually confident, convinced that my ills were temporary. The future would be different.

5

My two chief attachments during my years at Cambridge and immediately afterwards were for a girl called Jane Price and a young man called Stephen Carpmael. I was in love with them simultaneously. Both were more serious than former attachments, because both were declared. Both ended unhappily, but were all-absorbing while they lasted. They were long drawn-out, profoundly felt and suffered, non-violent. They wove themselves into the texture of everyday life, occupying all my thoughts and attention. In point of time the affair with Stephen reached its climax first. I can understand how young men come to ruin promising academic careers through total absorption in another person. At eighteen or so the emotions are perhaps deeper, more long-suffering and resilient than earlier or later. One feels oneself capable of greater joy, and hence of greater suffering.

The homosexual atmosphere at Cambridge was heightened by the fact that no secret was made of it. There were homosexuals well known for their open attachment to each other. I do not mean that it was widespread, but it was common enough especially in the more or less 'aesthetic' circle which I frequented. There were poets, good and bad, actors, even ballet dancers who made no secret of their disposition. I liked them; I responded to their undoubted good looks, sighing as usual to find I attracted none of them physically. They formed, indeed, a sort of freemasonry, and I dwelt on the fringe. My closest friend had indeed no trace of homosexuality. Others in my immediate circle had had homosexual friendships at school, of a passing kind. Two of my closest friends, Stephen and Norman, formed with me a triangular friendship, meeting in each other's rooms to talk into the night, or going out together on the river or the Backs in a punt. I can remember very clearly the moment of my falling in love with Stephen. It was in a punt on the river one summer's evening. It was in the third term of my first year. He had been at school with Norman, and I think their friendship had been intimate. But Norman was discovering that any homosexual tendencies he had had were superficial. Stephen, on the other hand, remained interested only in his own sex. (He never married, though he had a mild, maternal affair with a young married women while he was still an undergraduate.) He struck me as wholly charming, though I can see now that I idealised him. He was shortish, beautifully made, fair-haired and grey-eyed, his face drawn down from high cheekbones in an introspectively brooding melancholy. But he had a ready sense of humour and a good wit. He made out that he was constitutionally without any drive on account of a weakly childhood. He had a vein of flirtatious mockery which appealed to me. He had a quiet, gentle voice and was acutely sensitive.

As I watched him from my seat at the back of the punt, I became suddenly aware of the extraordinary beauty and grace of his movements as he slowly and rhythmically lifted the punt pole out of the water, dropped it in again silently and propelled us forward. He did it admirably, being a potential athlete. I looked at the warm flesh of his forearms, where the white sleeves were rolled up, and felt that such arms were worth dreaming of. Till that moment I had merely been fond of him in an affectionate, appreciative way. In a moment I was hopelessly in love. He became the fantasy lover of all my nights and days. We became close friends, he frequented my rooms more and more regularly. I asked nothing more than to be with him, I never dreamed that my attachment could have an outcome. I had at first no intention of declaring myself. I never saw him naked—I was not at first conscious of wanting to. I put him on a pinnacle of unattainability. The friendship continued and deepened; he read the same subject as I, he liked music, and we had much in common. I luxuriated in his presence, telling myself I found it enough.

I don't know how long the attachment to Stephen lasted—perhaps two years, perhaps into my third. But the atmosphere gradually became less dreamlike. Stephen began to have genuine homosexual attachments with known homosexuals. There was an actor who became very fond of him, there was also another young man on the edge of our circle, a nice-looking, not very intelligent boy. I learnt that they had a regular understanding, a sort of engagement. I became acutely jealous. In Stephen's room, and in his friend's, I found letters they had exchanged. I remember searching them feverishly for intimate revelations. I found only the kind of romantic confessions that might have been expressed in the first love letters of a boy and girl. What their relations were I could only guess. My jealousy reached fever-point and one evening, as he sat on my sofa, I confessed my love to Stephen. He was kind, sympathetic, understanding, and it was an unspeakable relief that he should know. But he didn't find me in the least physically attractive; and though he confessed he was touched and moved by my devotion, it could make no difference to his attitude. From then on he accepted my love but I became embittered that he could not reciprocate it. 'It's no good,' he said. 'You should have done something—something violent, but it's too late now.' I realised in an agony what he meant. His was such a feminine nature that he would, I think, have yielded to some kind of physical assault. Had I gone into my bedroom while he was in the sitting-room, stripped naked, returned and put my arms fiercely about him, he might have responded. For what my spectacled face could not do, my well-made body might have done. At all events I took his remark for a kind of challenge and pursued him round the room. He was more agile than I and easily evaded me. I sensed that he wanted a male ravisher, but this was not my rôle.

We remained friends, though after Cambridge we saw little of each other. I met him once and he told me he had taken a job as a schoolmaster in the West Country. His greatest delight was that one of his duties was to swim naked with the boys.

One vacation Stephen came to stay with me. We had plenty in common to make us good companions, even though our friendship was always touched with sadness for me. I had given up my bedroom to him and gone upstairs to a less comfortable attic room. When we were in pyjamas I came downstairs to sit by his bedside and talk. We talked on into the night, and I got cold. As I shivered, he invited me into his bed. Sheer pride, or some kind of fear, made me refuse, and I refused persistently; in the end he gave up asking me. The idle speculation that this episode evoked has never quite ceased to haunt me. Perhaps I was afraid of a passion to which such propinquity might drive me and I didn't want to be pitied or patronised by someone who had rejected me. I was always one to take no for an answer—a tendency I have too late learned to see as disastrous. It was almost as if I luxuriated in disappointment, as if I made for myself the image of the predestinately rejected lover.

My friend Basil, however, was pursuing heterosexual experiences with determination. He had a mistress whom I didn't find attractive on account of her bad skin. She was married and would slip away to spend weekends with Basil at Cambridge. She was devoted to him. In my last year Basil and I and some other friends got to know some girls from Newnham and Girton. I was extremely attracted to them, despite my attachment to Stephen. Indeed the homosexual side of my nature went into abeyance to some extent during my final year. I was utterly weary of celibacy and longed to cast off my virginity, which I found an embarrassment and a distress. A number of young women began to show an interest in me, but I was far too particular for one in my state. However, I was determined to make the effort to conquer someone by whom I could be physically attracted. In lectures I had noticed a girl with a good figure, a somewhat squat, high-cheekboned face and pretty blonde hair. She came to visit me in my rooms on the pretext of borrowing some books. I had not the least idea how to overcome my shyness in the presence of girls of my own age and she sensed this and gave me what I realised even in my innocence at that time, was an invitation.

'I was coming to a lecture in your college,' she said, 'so I thought I'd call in on that charming Richard Y—' From then on, all should have gone well. 'That's nice of you,' I should have said. 'Sit down and tell me why you find me charming.' But I was only twenty, and quite inexperienced. Given time, however, the relationship might have developed. But a moment later there was a knock at the door and Basil came in, evidently intending to stay. The girl made an excuse and vanished. When she had gone, Basil said something like, 'Whatever did that frightful girl come for?' I took this rebuke lying down. I didn't angrily defend the girl as I should have done, but in fact I was not sure what I thought of her. She was not frightful, certainly, but she was not my ideal either. I bore Basil a grudge for this which I have never entirely forgotten. Such are the small episodes that determine the direction of one's life.

The girl with whom I had my first serious affair was called Alison, a history student from Girton. She and her friend used to meet Basil and me and go on the river or share meals in our rooms. Basil at first directed his attention to Alison, but afterwards he dropped her, and she used to visit me alone. She was not in love with me at all. Her friend used to say afterwards that she came because my college had a good kitchen and I had a gramophone. She was extremely pretty, with the archetypal high cheekbones, clear skin and small, neat body.

One's first, clumsy attempts at love-making are probably something that no sensitive man recollects without shame. I felt I must make love to Alison—clearly it was expected. I thought I wanted it. I imagined that since she attracted me physically, I must be in love with her. I sat down beside her on the sofa, breathing heavily. I put my arms round her and kissed her. It was the first time I had ever done such a thing, and I was surprised to find how unexciting it was. I pulled up her jumper and began to caress her naked breasts. Having done this, there seemed nothing to do but to pull the jumper down again. 'I hope you didn't mind,' I said. She replied, 'I knew you would.'

The relationship continued. I found I wasn't passionately interested in Alison, nor did I have the capacity to arouse her. But I felt I must press on with my campaign and induce her to go to bed with me. A few days after our first encounter we lay together on my bed. It was a warm day and we embraced on the bedspread. I took off her jumper and bared her breasts—I didn't find them exciting. They were small and pinched-looking. I felt a sort of contempt for myself and a pity for us both, but I went on. 'Would you like to be my mistress?' I asked. What I meant was simply that if she wanted a real love-affair, I would take the necessary precautions and we would become lovers. She had no experience of this cold-blooded approach and imagined that I meant there and then. 'I don't want you enough—down there,' she answered. I took this to mean, not just that she was not in the least sexually aroused—I had done little to arouse her—at that moment, but that I was completely unattractive to her sexually. I never made the attempt again, though we had one more encounter. This is acutely distressing to recall, even now. I think she was at the time (that is, some six months after my last year at Cambridge) having a deeply unsuccessful love affair with an unscrupulous young man who took advantage of her infatuation and was unkind to her. At all events, when I went to visit her at Girton on a trip to Cambridge after I had gone down and she was in her final year, we were left alone by her other guests, and I automatically took her in my arms. We sat, and then lay, on her sofa. Suddenly she unfastened her skirt and took it off. She was asking to be seduced. I pressed my face between her legs, but was overpowered by the smell of urine. I felt no sexual excitement, only a sense of disgust.

I cannot quite leave the affair with Alison at that. My fault was that of ignorance, a lack of preparation for maturity. She was a nice girl, in many ways a sweet girl, and had it not been for the curse of my need for physical fulfilment, I could have had a close and rewarding friendship with her. Without realising it, however, I was trying to use her simply for physical gratification, without in the least knowing how to do so. She on the other hand had no illusions about our relationship. She taunted me, playfully, with 'putting too much into our friendship'. I was straining it beyond its strength; she was right. On the other hand I didn't want one of those calm, more or less surface relationships which can mean such a lot at the right time. I longed for passion, and was incapable of either arousing it or feeling it. Alison, like most women, was extraordinarily generous, ready to give. I was not ready either to give or to take. I saw little more of her, but I visited her friend in London, who was exquisitely beautiful—the only girl taller than I whom I have ever fancied myself in love with. I tried to seduce her, but failed miserably. She was unhappily in love with a tall, gangling man with protruding teeth, and I took her preference for him as an insult to me and as witness to the incomprehensibility of women. I had not the energy to pursue the relationship. It seemed that all I wanted was sex, and all that girls wanted of me was friendship.

Among the closest of my parents' friends during my adolescence and early manhood were the Prices. They were of similar nonconformist and teetotal beliefs. They also had a car, and because they lived in suburban London they liked visiting us at weekends to play tennis and bridge, to talk, have amateur musical and dramatic entertainments and enjoy other interests in common. The husband, a kind, ordinary man, was in business in the city, and they enjoyed considerable prosperity in the boom of the 1920s. His wife Doris, a romantic and cultured woman, was the driving force in the family. She told me afterwards that, as a young man, her husband had 'swept her off her feet'. She had been no more than a girl. I could never see him in this sweeping rôle, and I always imagined she had married him to get away from home. She told me this in order to underline what she felt to be his unsuitability as a companion for her. They had one daughter, Jane, a beautiful girl five years my junior, with whom I fell romantically in love and was always excited to see. They had

had a boy, but he had died at the age of six. Jane was ravishingly pretty, and her happiness was the main aim of the Price family. She read books, played the piano, loved music and was the ideal companion. I never could remember when I first fell in love with her. The feeling gradually increased, despite all other attractions until, about the time I left Cambridge, she became all-absorbing. The thought of her became obsessive, and after I had left behind the other romantic attachments of my university days, she became the object of my thoughts every day and night. It was as if my love for her had been building up over several years like a tide, and once there was no other attachment to hold it back, it surged into my consciousness and drove out all else.

One difference between a homosexual and heterosexual passion is that the latter is essentially a hopeful one, however remote the hope, because it carries with it the promise of fulfilment and fruition. A heterosexual passion seems normal, something to be proud rather than ashamed of, something that can grow and strengthen. The fact that nothing but the difference in our ages kept us apart was a spur to hope. At thirteen, living in the protected atmosphere of suburban respectability and nonconformity, Jane was naturally unawakened. I don't know if she was aware of the effect her beauty might have on the opposite sex; she was still a schoolgirl, absorbed in her books and her music, her riding-lessons and her foreign holidays with parents and friends. She was the ideal love-object for a secretive, scared and idealistic boy: there could be no danger in the relationship, if relationship it could be called. Moreover, I saw so little of her alone, and our conversation was so general, that I really had no idea what she was like. She could therefore be what I wanted to imagine her, the spirit of virginal sweetness, intelligence and sensitivity. I lulled myself into the belief that one day, in the fullness of time, she and I would naturally fall in love and begin the perfect marriage, enjoying a domestic happiness known only in the most unlikely romances. Meanwhile, at the time of my leaving Cambridge she was only sixteen. I was content to wait.

During my last year at Cambridge Jane's mother formed a passionate attachment to me which, had I been fully conscious of it, I would have found extremely embarrassing. She may at the time have been no more than thirty-six or so, an age at which a woman may reasonably form a passionate attachment for a young man of twenty-one. She was pretty, and all the men in my parents' circle were obviously attracted by her. She was gay, coquettish and pleasure-loving. The family would come down and have lunch with me in my rooms at Cambridge. In the winter we would sit and play my gramophone and in the summer we would go on the Backs. It was an idyllic time. In the holidays I would go and stay with the family near London, or put up there for the night if I had some engagement in town. My pleasure was always heightened by the fact that I was genuinely liked by the whole family. My visits were motivated by the desire to be near Jane. Her mother must have been well aware of my interest in her daughter, and she kept a wary eye on us. How could any mother do otherwise? But Jane was still at school—a London day school—and had homework or music practice every night; and she would be off to school in the morning almost before I was fully awake. However, I felt well rewarded by the glimpses I had of her and the conversations I managed to snatch before supper and breakfast.

I liked Doris and enjoyed her company as an intellectual companion, discussing books, going to matinées or concerts with her. On my side the relationship was one of pure pleasure, the kind of friendship with an older woman which can be so valuable to a shy young man. Inevitably, as the novelists say, her attitude to me changed, but I had no notion of its erotic nature until I thought about it later. She wrote me guardedly romantic letters, harmless enough but which would have betrayed to a more experienced eye a dangerously personal interest. I replied in all innocence, telling her of my thoughts and pursuits, and in equal innocence I left her letters neatly arranged in the paper rack on my writing table at home. In an access of jealousy, probably menopausal in origin, my mother, a considerably older woman than Doris, read the letters and wrote her a vicious denunciation. I never saw it, but Doris told me of it. My father had stepped in and smoothed things over—he didn't think my friendship with Doris was at all reprehensible. He was very fond of her and genuinely grieved that my mother should have behaved as she did. It was impossible after this to regard my relationship with Doris as not potentially dangerous, although I was so little attracted to her sexually that the thought did not worry me. I have, as I said, never been attracted to anyone my senior, and to me Doris was simply a good friend and companion and of course the mother of the girl I was beginning to be wholly obsessed by.

It was in some ways a strange situation. Doris's attentions to me, when we were alone, were becoming cautiously physical. She would lay a hand on my head and remark on the thickness of my hair. Another of her approaches was to stand in front of me with her back to me and say, 'I'm falling. Catch me.' I was obliged to put my hands under her arms to prevent her from falling. I was so innocent, I didn't know what she was up to. The reader might well conclude that I was sexually frigid, and perhaps I was. But it must be remembered that my inhibited upbringing would have rendered the thought of being sexually attractive to a married woman impossible. It simply did not happen, except in fiction and in sections of society with which I was wholly unacquainted. Not, I think, that this would have held me back, had I been attracted by Doris, but I was not. I was obsessed by her daughter, a fact of which she could not yet be fully aware. I was her friend, her confidant, her correspondent, her companion—a delightful companion because I was witty, interested in all that interested her, lively and well brought-up. When she steered the conversation into matters connected with sex, I was aware of some embarrassment, but not on account of any suspicion that she had any such interest in me. We were looking one day at a book of reproductions of academy pictures, and I chanced to open the page at a large nude. I betrayed my embarrassment, in the presence of a woman, by turning the page a shade hastily. She told me I ought to realise that the picture was very beautiful. She asked me one day if I would, as she put it, 'go the whole hog with a shop-girl'. I said I didn't know. She sighed, and as the conversation turned in another direction, Doris remarked: 'I'm a whole-hogger really.'

It is almost impossible to write of a woman such as Doris, after this lapse of time knowing all I know now, without sounding satirical and unsympathetic. She was basically a nice woman with a deep vein of unhappiness caused by her misalliance with a man so much her inferior in so many ways. He too was a good chap, in a golfing, suburban way. They were united by their nonconformity, teetotalism and their liberal views generally. But she felt the lack of an intellectual companion, and it was natural that she should take advantage of my need for such companionship to make emotional demands which I could not satisfy. There are two sides to every woman: one is the original, personal, individual woman who derives her strength from simply being herself; but there is also the side which needs, in every sense, to be fertilised by a man. Men are not complete without women, but they make a more satisfactory attempt at it. Women without men are unfulfilled, not perhaps in the deepest sense, but in everything that has to do with the life of the mind, the personality, day-to-day happiness. Doris lacked such company, but found it in me. I helped to awaken her spirit after it had come upon an arid patch when her only child had reached adolescence.

The child, too, needed awakening. I was too young, too immature, too egotistic and too ignorant to do this. I projected upon Jane my image of the perfect soulmate, the girl destined to be my companion through life, my wife, the mother of my children—not to mention the instrument by which I would ultimately lose my tiresome virginity in a spiritual-erotic consummation in the marriage bed. My thoughts of her were of course 'pure' in the extreme. I tried not to allow myself to think of her body. I only mentally undressed her when feeling tired, lonely and dispirited. After Cambridge I spent some time in a lonely bedsitter in London studying for my Civil Service exams. I solaced myself by keeping a confessional diary, filled mostly with unposted letters to Jane. This went on for a long time. The loneliness of my situation and the routine character of my work intensified my dependence on the image of Jane I had fashioned for my comfort. With her I was shy, but we were friends, excellent companions. The subject of love in relation to ourselves never arose between us.

As a result of my exams I was offered a post in the Indian Civil Service. I turned it down purely on the grounds that it would have meant separation from Jane. Later I took a post in England, but the Eastern offer was a blow. I was now twenty-three and Jane eighteen. The fever of my one-sided passion had now become so obsessive that I felt compelled to declare myself to her. I was absolutely ignorant of everything that can be described as courtship. I felt that courtship was something beneath the notice of the high-minded, totally dedicated lover, whose passion should be rewarded with immediate and wholehearted acceptance. It never occurred to me that she was unawakened, that she could not possibly have thought of me as a potential lover. The circumstances for courtship were not propitious. She was still at school, and I rarely had the opportunity of seeing her alone. However, I supposed that when I declared myself she would reveal that she too had been secretly in love with me for a long time and had hardly dared to hope, etc.

I have forgotten to mention that I had already told her mother of my feelings for Jane. Whether this confidence was motivated by a sense of honour or whether because I hoped in some way to enlist Doris' help I don't know. At all events I told her—perhaps six months before I declared myself to Jane. Doris took the news very coolly, revealing that she had never contemplated with pleasure the possibility of her daughter's marrying a member of my family. I don't know what was wrong with my family; perhaps she had social ambitions for her daughter. Undoubtedly the thought that my interest in her could be interpreted as a disguise for an interest in her daughter could not have pleased her—though she did not say so, and I would quite truthfully have denied it. She neither encouraged nor discouraged me. I told her that one day I would have to speak to Jane about my feelings, and perhaps I gave the impression that this would not be for a long time. I was embittered by the mother's very clear disapproval which, however, she came later to modify. I couldn't help noticing the contrast between the eagerness with which she would have had me as a lover and the lack of enthusiasm for having me as a son-in-law. She considered me good enough for a playmate for a married woman but not good enough for a husband for a girl nearer my own age. I never forgave her this.

The day came when I determined to speak to Jane. I was to go and stay for a night or two at the weekend. I was in a fever of impatience. My fate would be settled one way or the other. I don't think I had any doubt that she would accept my love. How could she not? I reached the house and was given tea by Doris. We chatted, then Jane joined us, but I was not left alone with her. We had supper, the four of us, for her father had also come home. At last, after supper, Jane went upstairs to get on with her homework in her bedroom at the back of the house. A few minutes later I found the opportunity to follow her. I went in and closed the door. There seemed little to say. As she stood up to greet me, I put my arms round her and held her close, but I didn't kiss her. At last my seriousness must have struck her. I had hoped for a yielding consent which would tell me silently of her secret love and unite our lives for eternity. No such thing happened. She gradually drew away, saying quietly, 'That's all. That's enough.' The sense of her words coming through to me, I said 'Do you mean for now or for always?' 'Always,' she said.

I accepted defeat. I spent the next few days, indeed months, numbed and shattered—not by my own foolishness and ignorance, as I should have been, but by her supposed final rejection, the blow to my pride and the collapse of the fantasy world in which I had for so long been living.

That any young man of twenty-three could have been so stupid, so innocent and so blindly uncomprehending as I was over Jane, I can still hardly believe. She was sweetness itself to me during the next few weeks. We corresponded: she regarded the correspondence as a substitute for the courting I should have given her. I regarded it as a hopeless masochistic going-over of lost ground. I told her of the diary I had been keeping. She asked to read it and I sent it to her. It is obvious to me now that she must have been deeply moved. She was a sensible girl, and we had a lot in common. Whether she would ever have accepted me if I had courted her like any other young man I don't know. However, she wrote to me very feelingly, and if I had known anything whatever about life and love, I could have felt extremely encouraged. After reading the diary she told me in a letter, 'I will do anything—*anything* you ask.' When I saw her a few days later, I said, 'You told me you would do anything I ask. I might have asked you to marry me.' She said with a sort of sweetly mocking gravity which I had for a long time known and loved, 'I knew you wouldn't.'

By no process of introspection can I understand my actions, or rather inaction, at this time. I can only ask myself a host of questions: Did I ever really want her? Did I want, or need, normal sex? Did I feel doomed to an interesting state of subjection to a ruthless and hostile fate? Was an essential narcissism my motive force? For I had grown up in the belief, despite my unacceptability in some respects, that I was a chosen spirit. All I desired would come to me without my making any effort, without my demeaning myself to court rejection. I was morbidly sensitive about the possibility of rebuff—this was part of my narcissism and pride. I was prepared to go as far as to put my arms about a girl, but after that I expected the rest to follow. She was supposed to collapse upon me in an ecstasy of love and gratitude.

But I doubt if there is any simple explanation—my utter failure (a failure which at the time of course I laid at the door of destiny in my fatalistic way) was no doubt the result of a chain of circumstances which would not be repeated precisely in the case of anyone else: my parents' puritan attitude to sex and normal relations between the sexes; my own narcissism caused by my having been spoiled and brought up to think I was in every way special; my romanticism derived from excessive reading of novels; my total ignorance of women caused by my having been jealously guarded from the company of girls except in superficial social contexts; my monastic boarding-school upbringing; my fiercely priggish attitude to sex and my lofty contempt for the ordinary processes of courting and love-making. Whether I should have been any happier if Jane had accepted me I cannot tell. The circumstances didn't then exist in which she could possibly have done so. Hindsight tells me that it would not have been very difficult to get her to accept me. I retired fatalistically into my conviction of failure and the sense that, while certainly some great future was reserved for me, I was destined to misery and loneliness. I read much, worked hard, saw the Price family from time to time, but did not again refer to my failure with Jane. I told Doris about it some weeks after. She was surprised that I had declared myself so soon, but extremely sympathetic and at the same time relieved. She told me I should have gone to the East—'Absence makes the heart grow fonder'—and that my love could have been gradually revealed by correspondence. But I am not patient by nature. If I cannot get something when I want it, I tend to accept the fact and lose interest. Not that I lost interest in Jane for several years. I hung on for a while in the vain hope that some miracle would occur to reverse my fate without my having to raise a hand. But it didn't. In time we lost touch with the family. Jane married a doctor and lived within reach of her parents in their London suburb. She had, I think, two children, but I never saw her again.

It is sometimes said that there are four women in every man's life: mother, first love, wife, mistress. My own life fits this pattern. Jane was, despite many infatuations, my first love, and even now her memory is suffused with a tender despair. I never knew or heard anything against her, I never saw or heard anything about her to dispel the illusion of her perfection. But first love is only half-love because it doesn't allow of any faults. I only know that, so far as I could tell,

Jane had developed no faults by the age of nineteen or so, her age when I last saw her.

All now are dead or lost to me—mother, first love, wife and mistress, and in my relations with all of them I see in retrospect the evidence and signs of my own failure. For a long time all that remained to me was the exercise of truth, the replacement of self-regard by self-realisation.

6

The three years or so that separated this first wholly committed love affair from my marriage were filled by uncertainty and despair. My main need and desire was for sexual fulfilment. It must be so for any young man who takes his virginity with him well into his twenties. All my friends, it seemed to me, had had satisfactory sexual experiences—I alone suffered under some sort of curse. During my year in London studying for the Civil Service I had a morbid and terrified interest in the prostitutes who solicited in the district where I lived. I had no intention of consorting with them, but they fascinated me. I knew instinctively that resorting to them was no solution to my problem, which was at least as much emotional as physiological. Moreover, I was particularly scared of getting venereal disease. So I suffered and was lonely and frustrated.

In the summer following my failure with Jane, I took a job as a schoolmaster at a boys' boarding school in Essex. I became thoroughly absorbed in the life of the place and was charmed by the boys, many of whom were in every way attractive. I formed secret sentimental attachments to several of them of the kind I had had at school. My keenest pleasure, though an infrequent one, was to supervise them in the swimming bath, where they bathed naked. I was not, to tell the truth, exclusively interested in boys at this time, though I was always responsive to their charm. One of them in particular I found attractive. I got him to call on me in my room in London later, where I took his photograph

At first I could not come to terms with the north London boys I taught, but quite soon I became extremely fond of them, enjoying their company, their jokes, and that maturity which is the mark of a true Cockney. There were boys I fell in love with at this school, but I cannot now particularise about any of them with much conviction. I loved many of them, and would curl up in bed with one of them in fantasy, night after night. They never suspected my feelings: there was nothing I could do to express them. While two or three of my colleagues were, I know, secretly homosexual to some extent, we never discussed the subject. They never revealed their tendencies verbally.

It was from this London school that two or three of my colleagues and I took some boys to camp in Dorset. The opportunities for sexual propinquity which this afforded were of course many. It was all delightful and yet futile. The idealised notion of the virgin male was enough to prevent any sensitive adult from showing his real feelings. Convention alone precluded any demonstration of these feelings, but I'm sure that every schoolmaster who joined these expeditions harboured suppressed homosexual feelings and enjoyed fantasy platonic relations with the boys of his choice. We never talked of it, and I'm sure the boys remained in blissful ignorance. What a world of kindness and help boys derive from the secret homosexual passions of their schoolmasters and scoutmasters.

During these years I was also looking for sexual fulfilment with a girl. I didn't find it. I imagine that a normally aggressive and sophisticated young man found as little difficulty then as his modern counterpart in securing sexual fulfilment. But the atmosphere was less permissive in those days, and in a conventional middle-class environment sex was ruled out, at any rate for some of us.

Another family with whom we were very friendly were the Craigs, who lived near us and with whom we played bridge and tennis, had meals and spent evenings of coffee and talk. We also met them at dances. Diana was the only daughter among four sons. She had a chocolate-box face with the complexion of a just ripe peach—there is no other adequate simile. Her body was classically beautiful, luxurious and well-formed. She had that kind of athletic tautness of physique which makes any young man's senses ache. Without,

I think, being herself oversexed, she aroused the almost open lust of every young man in the neighbourhood. She was also a very kind-hearted, easy-tempered, charming girl who frankly enjoyed the homage of young men, without special favour to any. She was, however, conventionally regarded as a dumb blonde—she was indeed almost silver blonde—with a very simple mind and low intelligence. Her brothers were academically brilliant and she was very conscious of this. Condescendingly, I allowed myself to fall under her spell, for which I despised myself as giving in to mere lust. I was of course wrong, priggish, self-defeating. At dances in each other's houses it became the practice to switch out the lights for quite long spells and dance in the dark. I would then, with expert sensual swiftness, turn Diana round, grasp her body from behind and caress her taut, rounded breasts. This gave me great pleasure, as it did her. She liked sensual caresses and if, when we were alone, I ever stood behind her, she would feel for my hands with her long cool fingers and draw them up over her breasts. I would never have thought of a serious affair, much less marriage, with Diana, and I came to despise myself for being sexy with a girl I had no respect for intellectually. There was also something against having a serious affair with a girl who had kissed every young man in the neighbourhood—it made her easy to get and cheapened her. But everyone loved Diana because she was without malice and, in a way, without coquetry. She was so frank about her fondness for men that she was incapable of archness.

I was, simultaneously, in love with one of Diana's brothers, also athletically built, smooth-skinned, classically featured. He liked me and looked up to me as his intellectual superior and his elder. At my Essex job I had acquired my first small second-hand car, and Diana's brother Duncan came with me one summer on a tour of Somerset. We walked, talked, drove. I was enchanted by his company, though we had, in reality, very little to talk about. He was still at a public school, and he wrote me long, long letters, to which I replied in full. Looking back on the friendship, I think he must have been fond of me, since he wrote such embarrassingly long (and rather uninteresting) letters. But he had no homosexual feelings towards me, nor, I am sure, towards anyone else. In Somerset we put up for the night at small hotels or inns. At one of these we were obliged to share a double bed and during the night I tried surreptitiously to come into contact, as if by accident, with the body of my bedfellow. Duncan was almost asleep, but he awoke, seemed surprised, and moved away.

I gradually got used to the idea that my rôle was to be the understanding friend of younger people, their confidant and confessor, giving all I could and getting in return only gratitude, homage, affection and respect. It was not in me then to make sexual advances to boys, or even to girls. It seemed as if I was to be content for ever with a kind of fantasy love, love at second-hand. The bodies of young men and women, which I yearned to caress, were to be for ever denied to me, like the shores of some unattainable island. I grew accustomed to this concept of my fate, falling gradually into a kind of despairing lethargy, making the most of second-best, living in my imagination a rich life of sensual gratification, failing more and more dismally in all contacts with the real world. I had myself no confidant. It was my fate to be alone: intolerable as this was at times, it had its compensations. I began to realise that I myself was the limit of my potentiality. No one would help me. Yet I believed in the miracle, the miracle that would yield the perfect relationship, give me the understanding, support and sympathy I needed.

After what I have said no one would imagine that my marriage could be a success. What do we mean by a success? All I need say for the present is that we remained married for thirty years until the car crash that killed my wife instantaneously three years ago. The shock was so profound that it left me without any direction or purpose in life. Only my wife's death has made it possible to realise all that my marriage meant to me. The price is too high, and I would gladly have avoided the knowledge if the cause could not have been.

Marriage is, to use the current phrase, its own message. If it lasts, it needs no justification, no explanation. A man and woman may superficially have little in common; they may differ over many things; they may quarrel. I will even say that they may be at constant loggerheads. Yet the fact of their being married, being together, transcends all this. Their relationship begins in misconception, illusion, misunderstanding, and persists through and because of the stripping away of illusion, the bitterness of realisation that the woman's conception of her husband and the man's conception of his wife are wrong and must slowly and painfully be replaced by the truth. Their marriage is not something which existed before they met each other; it is something that is created, as the participants are created, or re-created, by every moment of their being together. They are together against fate, against accident, even against their own natures. If they believe in marriage as a necessary relationship between two people for the sake, perhaps, of their children—whether this is stated or not—for the sake, perhaps, of companionship and combating the world together, the marriage will persist because of their faith in its rightness and inevitability. By this faith each is re-created from the ashes of his former self—not without any trace of that self—on the contrary, with the realisation that the former self existed only to evolve into the later self, as the pupa exists solely for the purpose of becoming the imago. Our marriage lasted till, and after, her death—that is the most important thing about it. I was of course fortunate in my marriage, despite differences that I once wrongly thought destructive.

I met Anne early one December at a party in London given by a mutual friend. I had heard much of her during the past two months, and my interest was aroused. She was attractive to men and 'worldly', as I was told by one whose judgement in such things I didn't trust. I therefore met Anne with keen anticipation. I was in the situation of one who was certainly looking for marriage, though nearly despairing of finding it. I was sick of loneliness, pointlessness; I wanted to settle down, have children, have a permanent companion who should belong to me and no one else. I shrink from using the word 'belong', but that is what we really all want. This applies to a woman as much as to a man. Each wants to belong and be belonged to. I also wanted a home of my own and an end to landladies' cooking.

Anne, as it chanced, was in the same situation, though she had reached it by a different route. She was in every obvious sense attractive: otherwise, perhaps, I should not have found her. She had had a number of affairs; she was not one to be for long without lover, or an admirer, a young man to take her out, make a fuss of her. She had had sexual experience, I fancy not very satisfying, but given her by sexually expert married men—one at least I knew of. There were probably others. She was not in fact over-sexed—on the contrary, I think she simply wanted to please. I never learned the details of her sex experience before I met her: I didn't want to hear about it, and she didn't want to tell me.

At this time I was very idealistic and what she once called 'chivalrous'. I wasn't interested in simply 'having an affair', though she would have agreed to it if I had wanted it. We would probably then have discovered our differences and separated. The marriage was to be a success because to me it had to be a success. I was too proud and too desperate to admit the possibility of failure. I was a puritan and Anne was sexually cool. She wasn't a passionate woman, she shrank from physical contact, even with our children. This doesn't mean she was emotionally cold, or that she didn't want and enjoy admiration. She flirted but kept people at a distance and the orgy of sexual abandon of which I had dreamed never took place. It might have done if I had had some experience before our marriage, but I was shy, nervous, clumsy, expecting everything to happen without effort. Later I learnt bitterly the extent of my foolishness and ignorance. We were, in a word, unsuited as lovers: but this, I lived to discover, hasn't much to do with unsuitability for marriage.

At the party where we first met we joked, exchanged bawdy stories and drank a lot of beer. It was one of those rather bohemian parties enjoyed by young people without much money. I thought to myself briefly, 'She'll do'—a comment the ungallantry of which still gives me a shiver of shame. But for me that was very high praise, since after all only the best would do. She told me long afterwards that she too, at that party, told herself I was the man she would marry. She worked in London in a succession of jobs as a shorthand-typist secretary and she lived in a one-room flat in Kensington.

Our courtship was conventional; we met once or twice a week either in her flat or at a restaurant or theatre. We had not, I discovered later, many tastes in common, but I thought we had, as she was so willing to be interested in anything I was interested in. She suffered, I later realised, from a deep sense of intellectual inferiority. Living with me improved her in the ways in which her education at a conventional school had not. Living with her also improved me in worldly matters, but not enough. I remained intolerant of many of the people she was happy to know.

Two months after I met Anne, I asked her to marry me. She accepted. There followed the usual family visits of inspection, talk of wedding presents, a house, and so on. I felt I was being taken to see too many aunts whom I had nothing to say to. I protested on one occasion, and Anne was furious and suggested we break it off. In a panic I said no, nothing would make me. I broke the news of the wedding to my mother by phone, saying I was bringing down Anne for the weekend and was going to marry her. It was a brutal way of doing it, but I realised afterwards why I had done it like this. Instinctively I knew there would be opposition, so I presented *a fait accompli* with which my mother must know she would have to live. She had unconsciously contrived to oppose every other relationship that had previously shown signs of developing between myself and a possible wife. She was anxious that I should marry and have children, but it had to be a girl to her liking, and naturally no girl could live up to her ideal of the wife for me. Instinctively, she tried to educate Anne into being the ideal wife. Anne was 'worldly'; she had an office job and liked a 'good time'; she represented the sinful, pleasure-loving 'fast' world which my parents had shunned with distaste and even horror. Anne also used too much make-up. A naturally rather pale girl, she felt unable to cope with London life without using rouge and other cosmetics which, to my mother, smacked of worldliness.

Nevertheless, the relationship between mother and wife worked because both wanted it to. My mother was deeply conventional and any suggestion that she was subconsciously trying to wreck our marriage would have been indignantly repudiated. Yet Anne had a battle to win, and in the end she won: but all battles are corrosive and wasteful. They reached a *modus vivendi*, though my mother could never forgive Anne for not being domesticated and not being enslaved to my needs and comforts. But she later had grandchildren whom she adored, and that was a lot.

Sexually, my wooing was fumbling and humiliating. Not that we didn't enjoy many warm and happy hours simply lying in each other's arms, but it seemed as if any attempt on my part to do more than this was destined to fail. One week-end towards Easter, when it was bitterly cold, we went down by car to a cottage lent me by a friend. On the way I called at a chemist and bought a packet of contraceptives, something I had never before had occasion to use. I felt that they were called for. When we got to the cottage I lit an oil stove in the bedroom, and we undressed and lay down together. It was very cold and I was far too nervous and anxious to succeed. I remained impotent—a bad beginning to our sexual relationship. Anne didn't criticise me in any way, but such things hurt one's pride and do much to damage a relationship from within. I am now convinced that no man has a right to marry until he has had sexual experience, although I was brought up to believe precisely the opposite. My mother later hinted that my father had also been a failure on their honeymoon and I'm not surprised. After this incident Anne and I tacitly decided to wait until we were married. I am also convinced, in extenuation of my own inadequacy, that if a woman has sexual intercourse with an experienced man and then marries an innocent, she runs into certain danger.

The same thing happened years later to my mistress, who married a virgin of her own age after I had been her lover for two years.

In my pride I often told myself that Anne was destroying me, but later I came to see how false this was. I destroyed her equally—I the worldly Anne, she the self-centred, success-obsessed me. Out of our mutual destruction was born a new unity, and out of that emerged our children, people in their own right, owing much to each of us separately but perhaps more to the union of us two collectively. It is almost impossible not to create a false impression of such a relationship. What I say in criticism of Anne must be seen as the reflection of what, as a naturally egocentric human being, I felt to be true of her at the time. In criticising another on whom one depends, one is to some extent expressing one's own sense of failure. In particular she had a great talent for friendship with people whom I thought boring and inferior, and most of our differences were about this. I felt that to spend time with such people was to debase and violate my own personality. Perhaps an ideal husband is one who is willing to do this, but I could not. I have always lived intensively in day-to-day things and I couldn't draw myself away from a situation in which demands were being made on my interests and my personality which I didn't feel able to give. Had I been a greater egoist, or less of an egoist, our day-to-day life would have been smoother. But to say this is to give a false picture of our marriage as one of constant tensions and differences. We had many hours of mutual pleasure in all sorts of things—visits to places of interest, foreign travel, the enjoyment of books and music, mutual pleasure in the society of people we both happened to like. There was plenty of that. Only when I was expected to be nice to boring visitors who had formerly been Anne's friends did I become dissatisfied and sullen. If Anne was not going to be the adoring, uncritical wife whom every man craves, I was not going to be the hospitable host and friend to a lot of time-wasting and, to me, frivolous people. I must have been in some ways a bitter disappointment. Loyalty to her old friends was a cardinal point with Anne, but I refused to be subjugated to it.

Five months after our first meeting Anne and I married. The service, the relations and friends, the champagne, the presents—everything was in traditional Kensington style. There were no speeches, no pomposity. Anne and I had a lot in common—in particular a dislike of pompous formality and a love of jokes and bawdy songs. I have often wished that, in a marriage such as ours, sex had not been regarded as the chief, or at any rate the first, thing of importance. I wish we could have lived together carelessly for some months and drifted into sexuality. But then perhaps we should not have married at all. At all events, sex became the most important thing in our lives once we had married, although I don't think either of us was especially interested in sex at that particular moment. In sex I was a hopeless failure, and such experiences are traumatic. My own failure to arouse Anne to passion and her apparent impassivity humiliated me on our honeymoon and convinced me that the marriage was a mistake. My attempts at physical intimacy in the hotel bedroom were clumsy and ineffective. I did what I thought was expected of me. A woman is, I believe, the lover her lover makes her, and I was incapable of making Anne the passionate, tender woman I imagined my wife would inevitably be. I am convinced, however, that she was not naturally 'sexy'. She was not spontaneously warm towards me at any rate, though I don't say she would have been the same with another man. On every occasion when I needed to be caressed, aroused, mothered, she failed me—or so I told myself. Yet she was a more generous person than I, more unselfish, kinder, more considerate. Perhaps she was able to be these things because she lacked passion.

Our honeymoon lasted a week, and at the end of it I told myself, almost calmly, that I had made the biggest mistake of my life and I had to live with it.

7

The story of Anne's and my accommodation to each other is a long and painful one. We were basically fond of one another. We had much in common in an intimate, though not sexually intimate way, and our accommodation was based on the tacit understanding that there is more to love than sex, more to sex than physical relations. Three years and more were to pass before our lives, like those of so many others, were altered by the outbreak of war in 1939. We went abroad together twice before the birth of our first daughter in the year before the war. Our first holiday abroad together was in Germany in 1936. We went to an idyllic valley where we stayed at simple hotels, eating, sleeping, walking, sight-seeing. We fell into a routine by which, after our midday meal, I would go to bed with Anne, enjoy a kind of lazy, sensual intercourse, leaving her sleeping in our huge feather bed in our big, hot room, and go for a walk round the village while she slept. This went on blissfully for the whole fortnight. We were very happy. We agreed to avoid having a child, so as to get to know one another properly. This we did successfully for eighteen months.

As I write, I am aware that the reader will know less of my wife than of others in my story. We established a profound intimacy based less on physical proximity than on a shared response to people, places, things. Above all, we were amused by the same things. Without this, it seems to me, our relationship would have been shadowy, almost insubstantial. Our life together, which lasted over thirty years, might be summed up in a series of infinitely subtle family jokes, developing into a series of words and phrases which we never forgot and which formed a sort of cumulative folklore existing only between us and later, to some extent, our children.

For the time being, however, I was coming to know my wife through the contact of our bodies, which remained, nevertheless, in a sense strangers. I enjoyed our afternoons together: the courting, the excitement, the penetration, the spasm, the contented aftermath: I don't know if these encounters satisfied Anne. They left her drowsy, perhaps fulfilled, I don't know. They did not represent the longed for ecstasy of sexual fulfilment so far as I was concerned. They represented the most satisfactory experience I could expect from the person whom I imagined physically, to be the wrong woman. It did not, at that time, matter. I was unsatisfied, I was unfulfilled, I was obliged to seek fulfilment and satisfaction in my work. Meanwhile I felt that as a man I was at least justified; that was what sex was, not so overwhelming and transcendent as I had imagined.

It was only much later that I came to regard sex and marriage as a battle. At this time I thought of it as peace and fulfilment. Anne thought differently, as if by instinct. I hadn't seen it then as a mental process of mutual attrition. I hated quarrels—I would do anything to avoid them. She, it seemed to me, sought them, as if to prove my manhood. She wanted to lose; I did not want to win. On one occasion, staying in London with her parents, I remember she started what seemed to be some trivial row in the bedroom. It ended in violence, with her hurling a pillow at me. I felt humiliated, worsted, without the satisfaction of victory. I had lost hopelessly, and by that loss I felt diminished in her eyes. She was the master, and this I resented deeply. Sometimes she accused me of a lack of spontaneity. She said once she wished I would take her, sexually, with violence, overwhelmingly, and with no contraceptive precautions. I never, as the saying is, 'let myself go'. I was always cautious, never spontaneous. Contraception is the enemy of spontaneity or, at any rate, it was in those days. I have always been too calculating, too prudent, too insistent on being, so far as possible, in charge of my own actions. I don't know why. At the root of it, I suppose, is fear, fear of the unknown in my own personality.

The unspoken battle between Anne and my mother went on. On one occasion my mother harmed her cause by hinting that it was time she was made a grandmother. This to me seemed vulgar, and allied me more deeply with Anne. Whether or not we had children, I felt, was our business, no one else's. I think I was right in assuming that the husband-wife relationship is unique and doesn't exist solely for the procreation of children, which I had always regarded as a by-product of marriage, not its purpose. In this I feel sure I was at one with Anne. We both wanted children, thought it was natural and inevitable, but refused to treat ourselves as mere organs of self-reproduction. In due course Anne became pregnant, the most natural thing in the world. Our first daughter was born a year before the outbreak of war. We adored the child, and our relations with each other remained happy. Quarrels were incidental. We never seriously disagreed about the upbringing of our children. I don't think either of us was emotionally greedy. This first child being a girl, I think Anne realised that I was entitled to a special relationship. And yet Sarah never became for me a substitute for Anne. We lived together, in harmony, with plenty of day-to-day friction, but nothing of much consequence.

The shock of the outbreak of war in 1939 was such as to make me sexually impotent. I may be quite wrong in ascribing this to the War, but the reality of it cannot be denied. Although, as in the previous years of our marriage, I tried to gratify my wife and myself sexually, I never achieved an erection. My humiliation was profound, and I underwent something like despair, wondering if the condition was permanent. Outwardly, our domestic relations had not changed and yet whenever I embraced Anne sexually, the result was sheer humiliation.

This went on for four years, towards the end of which my wife, quite justifiably, virtually accused me of being impotent. At this time I was in fact going through an intensely homosexual phase. Whether the homosexuality caused the heterosexual impotence, or whether the latter was caused by the shock of the War, I cannot tell. I remember that the actual outbreak of the War found us in bed together. The air-raid siren sounded. I could not from that time on give myself or Anne any sexual satisfaction. I can't explain this, I can only record it.

The outbreak of the War more or less put an end to the activities of the firm I was working for. On marriage I had decided that my prospects in schoolmastering were poor, and so had given it up and taken a job with an advertising agency. Accordingly, I applied for whatever jobs I was qualified to carry out in the neighbourhood. The remnant of my firm went to the Lake District, but Anne and I were unwilling to go there. I took a job teaching at the local grammar school, whose staff had been depleted by the call-up. Being qualified at least by the possession of a university degree, I was given the job.

I succumbed happily to the charm of the young, virgin male eager for experience, innocent of evil, lively, intelligent, wanting friendship and love. Many of the boys I taught were physically attractive; even those who were not had something youthful and appealing about them. I fell in love collectively with my classes and in particular with certain boys of extreme beauty. When they were absent, I missed them. When they were seated in front of me, listening or answering, reading or writing, there grew up between us a subtle and secret love which cannot easily be described. Boys always know the difference between the masters who simply do their jobs and those who have a natural concern for them. I was always liked, mostly loved, because with me their interests always came first. I had the ability to interest and amuse them. They responded spontaneously and warmly. What I meant to them of course was different from what they meant to me. I was, I suppose, a benevolent father-figure, though considerably younger than their own fathers—perhaps an elder brother figure. I was never without interest or concern for their personal wellbeing. I gave them much. Without the sexual interest on my side, perhaps I could not have given them so much. They, on the other hand, represented to me ideal loves, pastoral creatures, nymphs, the objects of secret love in fantasy, always present, always unattainable. The youthful beauty of their faces and hands, the grave sweetness of their eyes as they looked at me, the charm of their bodily movements—all these were a sort of sacred grove of pagan experience, known only in fantasy, never in reality.

The concept of homosexuality, the image of the 'queer' schoolmaster, did not then exist. I doubt if it was discussed or even known about among schoolboys of the wartime period. It is an idea that has gradually filtered through to the public, through the press, through the permissive context of postwar society. If those boys had been as aware of it as their sons are today, they might have guessed my secret. All the same, I was then so secretive, so correct and concealed, that I think they would not have guessed. Yet in their way they were guilty too—if 'guilty' is the right word. They flirted with me, in the sense that by being attractive or amenable or demanding, they drew to themselves my interest and attention. They made fun of me, they 'saw how far they could go', in being cheeky or disrespectful or inquisitive about my personal affairs. A subtle love-relation developed between me and the most intelligent and attractive of my pupils.

I was very happy in my life at the school, and this happiness communicated itself to the boys; we were content in each other's company. No one who thinks of homosexuality as a crudely physical relationship can understand the subtlety and richness of Platonic love. In a relationship between a man and young boys, provided the boys are normally healthy and the master is reticent, there is a delicately sensitive, fluid relationship based always on potentiality, never on actuality. The boy is in fact saying. 'Would you like to touch me, to kiss me, to put your arms round me?' He is daring the master to some crudely physical act. The master is thinking to himself, 'I adore your young body; I would give anything to embrace you, to caress you, to kiss your young face and stroke your body, but we are civilised, there are laws. I cannot shock you, I cannot risk hurting your youthful sensibility and betraying your trust; I cannot appear as a beast in your eyes.' After all the boy is almost certainly not homosexual; he has the natural desire to attract the notice of an older member of his own sex on the condition that his youthful, reticent virginity is not outraged.

I never offended one of these boys. I claim no credit for this. I preferred that the relationship should remain in suspension, as it were. I could not offend or outrage by some overt physical act. It was largely pride on my part: I couldn't abide the thought of being snubbed, rebuffed or talked about, and the way to avoid a rebuff is to make no approach. Perhaps in my fantasy I imagined the ideal boy would make an overture to me and thus absolve me of responsibility. But it never happened. I have known at least two men who went to prison because they were unable to control their desires, as I did. I have always been a coward in this respect—or at least until recently. Yet the ideal, as it were, pastoral relationship, the relationship of fantasy, of happy possibility rather than actual rejection, was at this time and has often been a source of delight to me. After all, was I not a civilised, decent man, knowing full well that physical relations with boys were out of the question? I accepted my fate: to love, to desire, to lust without physical fulfilment.

The most intense and tantalising satisfaction I achieved was during the year or so after the outbreak of war. It so happened that the master in charge of swimming was called up. I offered to take over on the two days of the week when the boys went to the local swimming baths after school. This was a purely voluntary affair, no boy was obliged to go to the baths—the thirty or forty who did so went of their own free will. I was the master in charge, who blew the whistle when it was time to stop, discouraged excessive horseplay, and presumably rescued the drowning.

The public swimming bath, reserved on two evenings a week for our school, was a severely functional building made of modern red brick and concrete. The water measured one hundred by thirty feet and was roofed over with glass. It was surrounded by concrete, which was in turn surrounded by cubicles. The doors of these cubicles were painted brown and were divided horizontally into two equal sections. Thus anyone changing out of or into a swimming costume could keep the lower half, or both halves, closed. Our boys were casual about their changing arrangements. On arrival they would take possession of the cubicles, strip off their school clothes and put on their regulation bathing trunks. These trunks covered their buttocks and genitals only, leaving their thighs and the lower parts of the back naked. A boy thus half-concealed, half-revealed was to me the most perfect object in creation—smooth-skinned, as a rule more or less hairless, strong, firm, supple and in some indefinable way virgin, helpless and vulnerable. Gazing with secret shame at their young beauty—in a way which I think would not be misunderstood nowadays—I was overcome by the desire to cherish and protect them. These young bodies seemed to me infinitely vulnerable and chaste. The rounded shoulders, straight backs and subtly shaped arms, the undulating, tapering legs, the rounded buttocks and the soft, hidden groin, genitals sometimes deeply hidden, sometimes prominent—all this made up for me a thing so unattainably lovely, so aesthetically perfect that it seemed to me infinitely pathetic that they were not to be held, grasped, caressed and protected, that only afterwards, in fantasy, could I fondle and caress one or other of my beloved objects, torturing and teasing myself with the simple but unbridgeable gulf between imagination and reality. The truth was that a boy's body was the most perfect, the most desirable, the most satisfying, the nearest, the most vulnerable, and yet the remotest and most unapproachable thing in existence. Why, I wondered, was it as impossible to go up to a naked boy and put my arms about him and say, 'I love you. May I caress you?' as to jump in front of a moving train or plunge one's hand into fire?

In my activities as master in charge of swimming, it strikes me that there must have been a strong element of masochism. I knew that to go twice a week to the baths, to see these young creatures nearly naked, was to impose on myself an exquisite torture of frustration. It hurt every moment, yet I was unable to refrain. I would myself enter a cubicle, put on a pair of trunks, descend carefully into the shallow end and swim cautiously towards the centre of the bath. I was a bad swimmer, but I enjoyed it because I was able to be in the same element as the boys.

Those swimming days were a voyeur's heaven. How I would gaze and gloat as the young, slim bodies slipped into the water or lolled on the side, ran along the concrete or climbed the diving boards and precipitated themselves into the water. Partly, of course, my feelings were mixed with envy: I had always been a physical coward, and I hadn't learned to swim until I was eighteen. These young athletes had something godlike and indestructible in their swimming and diving abilities of which I was quite incapable. I loved all the boys in the water, but I had my favourites. There was one sturdy, well-made boy whom I adored and who knew I loved him. He flirted with me shamelessly, cheeking and making fun of me. There was another, black-haired and beautifully proportioned, a superb diver. There was a big, outrageously beautiful boy, the son of a Welsh miner. I asked why his family had moved from South Wales, and he told me it was because his father had not wanted him to go down the pits. I see him now, standing on the edge of the concrete, about to dive in, his big, concealed buttocks quivering before he leapt in. There was a boy I didn't greatly like, with a somewhat boringly handsome face and low intelligence: but his body was breath-taking. He stripped like the traditional Greek athlete. If there is such a thing as perfect classical proportion, this boy had it; there was not half an ounce of spare flesh on his lean, muscular body. It was impossible for me not to spy on him as he dried his body in the cubicle after swimming. He became aware of my attention and covered himself. I longed to say: 'Just let me gaze at you, naked, and I will be happy.' As it was, my attention was furtive but not unnoticed. He was, I think, the only boy I succeeded in embarrassing.

Perhaps my secret favourite was a slim, rather bony boy

6—AOAE * *

with fair hair and a pale, almost unformed body. His face was girlishly curved and chaste, with the high cheekbones, grey eyes and placid, quiet brow; he was full of fun, and he loved me sincerely. He spoke in a beautifully grave, sensitive voice. After swimming, he would sit beside me on the bench at the side of the bath, talking idly and joking about the boys in the water or about other masters. He was not conventionally attractive, but to my eyes and heart he was perfection. I longed to consign the rest to oblivion, much as I loved them, and to be left alone with him; to hold him in my arms and say soft words and stroke his young, angular, virginal body. I think he was aware of my secret adoration, and accepted my gazing at his naked arms and legs and breast as a kind of innocent worship. If he was aware that I lusted for him, he trusted me perfectly, knowing I could never hurt him. Long after he had left school and the War was over, he wrote to me. I tried to get in touch later, wondering what he would be like at thirty, but I never saw him again. Towards the end of the War, as a young member of the cadets, he was detailed for fire-watching duties at the school on a night when I also was on duty. We talked, and he told me how all the boys loved me. The scene that enacted itself in my fantasy continued with my saying to him, 'And you, Vivian—do you love me? Do you mind if I kiss you?' and my arm would go round his shoulder and I would draw him to me. Looking back now I suppose, had I been a corrupter, it would not have been difficult to corrupt him.

My decision not to make any physical approach to the boys I so much desired had little to do with moral scruples. It was mainly prudential. I knew that if I approached any boy, however gently, he would talk: I should soon be known, not as the decent, interested schoolmaster who laughed and talked and swam with them, but as a nasty man who messed about with boys. It was as simple as that. No boy ever came to harm through me. I respected them; I respected their chastity and their shrinking from unwanted notice. They never, so far as I knew, exposed their genitals when changing back into their clothes. They were young animals but instinctively conscious of their unaroused sexuality. My days at the swimming baths were happy ones, not because I was close to the boys as I would have liked to be, but because I was as close as was possible. I was approved of, I was liked, and my desires remained secret. My fantasies about my favourite boys were enacted later, after I had gone to bed. Then I had all the liberty to embrace, to caress and fondle, to kiss or to hurt as the fancy took me.

The Deputy Headmaster of the school once caned a boy in my presence in the staffroom. He was not beautiful, but he was an attractive boy, always in trouble but well-liked by the other boys and most of the staff. He had a good skin and was on the chubby side. He was made to bend over, and his buttocks in their grey flannels presented a wonderful target to the sadistic master with the cane. The cuts—I forget how many—were well-aimed and vicious. It was clear that this master was enjoying himself. As the boy left the room, I could see that he was in great pain. His face was flushed and his eyes full of unshed tears. I felt a profound pity and an intense fascination. I have always longed to administer corporal punishment, yet always been thankful that it was not in my power to do so. On the few occasions when I have sent a boy to be caned, I always felt guilty and hatred for myself.

My interest in flogging grew with age. At the time of which I write it was limited. I loathed flogging with the fanatical hatred of a man who longs to practise it. This may well be hypocrisy, but I feel sure that it's better to act out one's sadistic impulses in fantasy only, as once, as a child, I acted out masochistic impulses in fantasy. I never saw a boy caned naked, but I always longed to. Boyhood romances, such as those of Rafael Sabatini, in which floggings occurred on ships, were always precious to me, and the pages where such accounts could be found I read again and again with gloating fascination. I can't account for this fascination, which was almost as strong as sex itself.

As I have said, I never caned a boy, only a contemporary,

and that by mutual agreement. For a long time I both regretted and was glad of this. All or most of the flagellation in my experience has been vicarious. The Headmaster of the school where I taught during the War would cane boys in his study—not excessively or viciously but, I think, with quiet satisfaction. Some of the staff even complained that he was weak and too often told the wrong boys to go away and not annoy Mr So-and-So again. I used to teach in a room adjoining his study and separated only by a closed door. It was not uncommon for my lessons with a small section of the sixth form to be interrupted by a murmur of voices followed by a succession of four or five cuts with the cane. Through a closed door a flogging has a particularly dead and mechanical sound. There is no swishing noise, only the sharp sound of the cane as it cuts into the stretched bottom. Another feature of caning which is integral to its fascination is the mental picture it offers of the purple weals, the twin marks made by the cane as it hits both buttocks with equal force. The swollen ridges are an object of aesthetic satisfaction. Why, I wonder? It is a mystery.

On the occasions when these canings occurred, there was an atmosphere of peculiar embarrassment among the boys I was teaching. No one said anything, but there was a feeling of constriction, as if every boy had a lump in his throat. We all got on with the lesson in a casual manner, as if nothing were happening, but the fascination of all could be felt.

The Headmaster deteriorated considerably as a result of the strain of the War; he became absentminded and vague. He was getting old and tired and he didn't give himself enough to do. One day he said to me, 'I like something to do in the afternoon, even if it's only to tan a boy's backside.' Yet he wasn't by nature a vicious or cruel man. He never, so far as I knew, caned simply for the pleasure of it, but if he felt he had to, he enjoyed it.

I once reported two boys for misconduct. One was a coarse, vicious boy who circulated the vulgarest pornography secretly in the classroom; the other was a decent, attractive boy, foolish and gullible rather than actively insubordinate. It was this boy who had his bottom caned, while the other escaped, though he was clearly the instigator. I never after that reported anyone to the Headmaster, whose judgement I could only despise.

It is only a matter of time before caning is abolished in public schools, as in state schools, but it still persists with remarkable tenacity, proving that it is enjoyed by schoolmasters—perhaps as a compensation for their way of life.

It is sometimes argued in favour of the retention of caning that boys approve of it and prefer it to other forms of discipline. It's all over, the argument goes, in a short, sharp burst of pain, and everyone is satisfied and makes a new start. That many boys are fascinated by it, and indeed perhaps even welcome the submission to a respected, even a loved schoolmaster, is undeniable. What they don't realise is that, in offering a usually private part of their bodies for the gratification of a cruel or sadistic adult they merely perpetuate the cruelty and encourage this form of sexual gratification. If any man habitually canes without some stirrings of sexual desire, he is not a full man. If this were just one form of discipline, such as the loss of liberty or the repetition of some tedious task, why all the prurience, the secret interest, the private discussions, the reticence and embarrassment? Why the continuation of interest into manhood among those who were beaten at school? It is the only form of punishment in English schools which becomes a subject of lifelong interest. I can't forget a drawing I once saw in a public lavatory thirty years ago. It wasn't the usual coarse graffito, but a most artistically executed pencil drawing of a naked youth with flogged buttocks, and under it was written, in the educated hand of an art student, or so it seemed, a concise and graphic account of what 'I' would like to do to 'you'. 'I would strip you,' the narrative ran, 'lay you over my knees and beat you lightly with thin twigs until your buttocks were red, tender and inflamed. Then with a thicker cane I would administer six dozen hard, sharp cuts to the prepared surfaces.' It was all fantasy, but it was very vividly realised.

Part of the fascination of flagellation is the self-disgust it produces. I was once obliged to witness a flogging, by the Deputy Headmaster, of a wretched boy with red hair and a rat face who had no attractions whatever. He was poor, and an habitual offender against school rules. It was I who had got him this beating. The boy took his punishment with stubborn indifference. My self-disgust was acute, as the boy bent down in a shaft of wintry sunlight and clouds of dust rose from his grey flannel trousers at each stroke of the cane. The boy was later killed in the War. He had joined the Navy at the first opportunity, and his ship was sunk by a German submarine.

8

The period of the War and the two years that followed were emotionally barren, devoid, that is, of climax and excitement. I led the conventional life of a married man, and the father of first one, then of two children. My sexual relations with my wife were restored after the years of sterility and never again suffered a total eclipse. We were not passionately in love, but we were both still young, and sex came naturally, if infrequently. I never dreamed of infidelity. Deviations in fantasy with boys were one thing—they were my secret and my wife, I am sure, never guessed at them. But infidelity with another woman never occurred to me until some time after the War, when I reached the age of thirty-nine or forty.

A change of job followed the War. I left teaching and joined a business establishment, not unlike the one I had left at the outbreak of war. There were young women about, and the intense atmosphere of a boys' school was replaced by a more normal one. I think this was partly why my homosexual interest gradually dwindled, to be replaced by a specifically sexual preoccupation with young women. I stress the word 'young', because it is crucial. I had been interested in boys rather than men. Now I began to be interested in girls, as distinct from women. I remained, in my imagination, a man of eternal youth: my wife had aged, but I had not. I began to look with interest at young women half my age, the same age, that is, as I had been when I was in the pride of sexual vigour. I began to hanker after a sexual relationship in which the unhappy experience I had had with my wife, the frustrations caused by my own inadequacy, would not again count against me. I knew more about women now. I had learned from my mistakes with Anne. I wanted a fresh start, but not with my wife—that was out of the question. Above all, I wanted some young and beautiful creature, virginally feminine, to want me passionately, to give herself to me unconditionally. All this was more or less fantasy, and not allowed to enter the field of possibility. I was still at this time wholly dedicated to the idea of fidelity. All my puritan upbringing and my attitude of chivalry towards my wife, as a companion and mother of my family, inhibited any thought of infidelity. I was fatalistic, regarding myself as eternally doomed to my present way of life, emotionally dead and resigned.

I have never recovered from my sense of guilt in the ensuing years. Yet the irony was that whereas I regarded infidelity as the prelude to an inevitable final break, my wife would have accepted it provided there was no final break. She had seen enough of the world to know that such situations existed between thousands of married couples. To me it was a case of all or nothing.

I began to see myself growing first middle-aged and then old without ever having had a full, passionate sexual relationship with a woman. The strain began to tell on me, and I became restless and desperate. At the age of forty—a time when similar things happen to many men, though I did not then realise that the pattern was classic—I fell spontaneously and passionately in love. It was as if I had suddenly returned to adolescence. We were performing a staff play at work and I was the producer. It was necessary to rehearse after working hours. A girl called Denise had been chosen for a small but key rôle, and from the first I found her attractive. She had a certain airy, boyish grace, with very dark eyes and very fair hair. Though I didn't realise it at the time, she was making a set at me, greeting me with a shy, maidenly smile and making light, coquettish remarks when we met. She was, I discovered, completely hard as far as I was concerned, but she was flattered by the obvious admiration of a senior member of the firm and the producer of the play; it clearly gave her status in the eyes of the other girls. It happened also that there was a preponderance of girls over men in the firm, and although she had friends outside, her working hours were rather bereft of men.

One evening we passed on the stairs. I greeted her with no more than a conventional 'Good evening, Denise', and when I reached my room I realised with a shock that I was madly in love with her. I made no plans; I certainly didn't think of running away with her. I thought only of making love to her and possessing her, whatever the consequences.

We parted for the Christmas holidays, after the production of the play. I spent the holiday oblivious to any other thought but that of Denise. What I hadn't realised then was that in an affair between a married man and a girl less than half his age, it is the girl who takes the lead. If she wants the affair, it will prosper. If not—if she only wishes to flirt and preen herself in the man's admiration—she will do just as much as is necessary to retain the man's interest, without involving herself an inch beyond what she considers prudent.

At the end of the holiday I was in a fever to see Denise once more. I knew that I must make my feelings known. I had no idea how such an affair had to be conducted. I wouldn't flatter her with presents and invitations, since I regarded this kind of behaviour as beneath the dignity of such a love as mine. I had the notion that such things would only have been insults.

I had managed to have Denise transferred to my immediate office. She became in fact the girl who did my shorthand and typing. She noticed this attention of course, and reciprocated it with small attentions of her own—letters posted, a handkerchief found, a private telephone call arranged, a button stitched on. It intrigued and amused her.

Then one evening, when on some pretext I made her stay behind after office hours, I declared my passion with as much clumsiness as if I had been a schoolboy. I forget the exact words I used, but I told her I loved her, held her at arm's length and drew her slowly towards me. Adroitly and coolly she turned her lips to one side, so that my kiss landed on her cheek. I held her for a few moments and then let her go. What did one do next?

'I love you,' I said. 'I want you terribly.'

She said nothing, her head lowered, completely mistress of the situation. She waited for what would come next.

'Do you mind my kissing you?' I asked—a question which must at any time be one of the most foolish that can possibly be asked.

'I do really,' she answered in a cool but not unfriendly tone.

Presently she sighed, picked up her handbag and said she must be going.

'I'll see you tomorrow,' I said.

She didn't answer, but disappeared with light, athletic steps.

I thought of nothing but this incident until I saw her again. I felt doomed, as if I were pursuing a course which had been dictated to me by some outer force. The Denise I dreamed of at night and when I woke in the morning was half fantasy, half reality. I endowed her with qualities she did not possess. She was, in fact, as I learned later, a rather commonplace, or at any rate ordinary girl, not long out of school and with a mind largely nourished on schoolgirl chatter and women's magazines. She was indeed at her most natural when telling me, as she sometimes did, in a friendly and confiding way of some schoolgirl escapade, charabanc trips on which she and her friends had made hilarious remarks to passing youths. Yet her ordinariness was veiled from me by my infatuation, which lasted perhaps six months. They were some of the most restless and intense months I have ever spent. I wasn't cut out for the pursuing lover. Had I known it, I expected her to fall in love with me and surrender without a struggle, as many years before I had expected Jane Price to. If she had done so, I have no idea what would have happened. As it was, I contrived to be alone with her as often as it was prudent. She had a pretty speaking voice, and I enjoyed talking to her and hearing her read out notes and memoranda. She knew I admired her and enjoyed my admiration, but she didn't relish my more physical attentions. When I kissed her she became indignant and flustered. We didn't talk about very much, mostly about her. On one occasion I put my arms round her and drew her to me. She resisted, got up and made as if to go.

'Sit down,' I begged. 'I shan't hurt you.'

She remained ruffled. I buried my head in my hands and groaned.

'Denise,' I said, 'tell me what you think of me.'

'Not very much when you act like that,' she replied with pert primness.

It wasn't her fault that her attitudes and her responses were suburban. I had no right to expect that she should possess the qualities with which I endowed her—a sense of tragedy, of struggling with a hopeless fate, a feeling of sharing with me a tragic fate. I don't know what I expected of her. I'm sure that if she had said, 'I adore you, but it's no good. We have to think of your wife and children', I should have been content to leave it at that. I certainly had no intention then of leaving my wife. Probably the affair with Denise was to be a tragic adventure—I couldn't tell.

I was lucky to have an old and confidential friend in Simon Chadwick—we had been friends for several years. He was considerably younger than I, but his regard for me and the interests we shared made us close. In particular he was always ready to be my confidant, to step in with sympathy, advice and practical help. I told him about Denise, and he listened with interest and concern. He was kind and tactful, but later I discovered he thought the Denise affair unsuitable and destined to fail. He never failed me, however, and was a loyal ally in all my difficulties, then and later, although I had placed him in an awkward position since he was fond of my wife and she of him.

At the beginning of my infatuation with Denise I was just forty years old. As the affair failed to prosper, I found myself in a fever of unsatisfied desire; I was like a raging animal. I had never experienced the complete fulfilment of sexual abandon; it was something I knew of and yet had missed. It seemed to me essential that I should have it. I craved complete physical submission to a young woman, a woman I had wrongly identified as Denise. This period, brief and hectic as it was, was unlike anything I had ever experienced, or have experienced since. I was unable to get out of my mind, morning, noon or evening, the image of a naked young woman entirely given up to yielding me pleasure and deriving pleasure from the contact of my body. How to satisfy this craving I had no idea. I used to escape from the flat and wander about the streets, hoping in some undefined way to meet someone who might gratify my compulsive sexual greed. I didn't want prostitutes, since I knew instinctively that they would not provide the satisfaction I needed. I wanted a willing and attractive partner of my own class, or near enough. It was a curious state of being. I made sexual advances to no one except Denise. She did not respond and I felt before long that she was not the solution of my problem and so unconsciously I began to look round for other possible women. I went to stay with my friend Simon in Cambridge. He had a large acquaintance there. I told him everything about my predicament, and he did his utmost to find me someone to sleep with. He was very good to me; he was genuinely concerned for my happiness and active in trying to satisfy my raging lust. I was of course at this time wholly and aggressively heterosexual. I had no interest whatever in my own sex.

Then I talked to my old and experienced friend Basil, telling him of my dilemma. He was equally understanding and practical. He told me that it had always been my failing to become fixated on a particular individual. He said he was delighted that I was, as he put it, 'on the warpath', and that exactly the same phenomenon had happened to him at the age of forty. (He was about two years my senior.) He implied that what I needed was a woman, and I must get out of my head the notion that it was any particular woman.

This advice proved effective. A few weeks later I realised that I was not in the least in love with Denise. I began to lose interest in her. I made up in my mind what I called a 'short list' of young women who would answer my needs, three or four of whom I had noticed in the office as being physically attractive and personally acceptable.

Among these were a girl called Barbara and another called Celia. Barbara was a sultry, country type with a sexy body and an obvious affection for me. At an office dance she brushed her cheek against mine, and I knew that she would need little persuasion. But I was already more attracted to Celia.

She also was a girl from the country, very quiet and beautifully spoken, with a soft West Country burr which appealed to me greatly. A woman's voice has always had for me—as indeed has a boy's—peculiar sexual attraction. I cannot imagine myself attracted for long to anyone with a harsh, shrill or rasping voice, whatever their bodily appeal. Celia had the complexion of a ripe peach, and the hair of a Titian model: not that I have ever been especially attracted to auburn hair. The colour didn't matter, but the texture was thick and soft. Her body was full, even fat with a kind of puppy fatness which she later lost. She was physically very fastidious and made herself as attractive as possible. There was in her quiet intensity, her brooding softness, the promise of infinite comfort and delight. She appeared cool, yet the intensity of her personality, both in her speech, and her movements, was always in evidence. She had a sense of humour, a sense of fun. She seemed made for tragic passion: this was exactly what I felt I needed. Her face was round, full, very clear-skinned. I can't remember her eyes, except that they shone with merriment. Her hands were small and neat, her whole body infinitely attractive. What she concealed, rather than revealed in any overt way, was her intense desire for a passionate relationship with some man of experience who would provide what she needed. Perhaps she unconsciously wanted the father who, in real life, she could not love. She had had many admirers, yet because she always chose those who had some streak of chivalry, she knew she could trust them not to force her to a relationship for which they were unsuited. In a sense she was what has come to be called a gerontophile. The type is common among women, less common, I think, among young men.

And so it was that Celia and I were as nearly as possible what each needed at that time. I had noticed her among her companions at the office, as any man must. She was not a flirt; as I said, she seemed cool and detached. It is, I have noticed, the flirts, the coquettes, who have admirers always around them. They love power and do not, perhaps, want passion. Passion involves giving, and Celia was of the kind that has much, indeed everything, to give. She wanted, she needed, to give herself to the first wholly worthy object she met. I was that object. For the first time in my life I had the peculiar exhilaration of being desired by someone whom I desired.

I have forgotten to mention an episode which occurred a few months before the present action of my story. It is one of those episodes that are perhaps of crucial importance in life, in the sense that destiny was at that moment decided, one way or another: had things gone otherwise then, they would have been otherwise thereafter. But since things are only the projection of people, it could not have gone otherwise.

In the extreme distress of mind that my infatuation with Denise caused me at the outset, I longed to confide in someone who cared for me, someone who could have made a difference. I loved my wife Anne, and have never ceased to do so; I had always enjoyed and valued her company both at home and on holiday abroad. Our only disagreements had been superficial and were mainly about people whose friendship she valued and I did not. In one important respect we had a close communion of views: we agreed about the upbringing and education of the children. I desperately needed her support in combating what threatened our mutual happiness. I wanted to tell her of the situation and ask for her help and advice. I found her sitting beside the fire one evening and sat beside her on the rug at her feet. I laid my head on her knee, hoping that she would put a hand on my forehead and ask what was the matter. It seemed to me that any woman would have known that something was very wrong with her husband. But she made no move, said not a word. I wanted her to ask what was wrong; to tell her that I felt an infatuation for this girl; to be appealed to let it go no further. Then I would have been magnanimous—I would have given it all up with one grand gesture of resignation. But this was not to be. From then on I knew I was on my own. I would have no ally in the fight that was to be waged. The conflict between Anne and me was a conflict to the bitter end, and only when I had lost was I to be forgiven. I had to face the bitter truth which Anne knew already—that a true relationship between a man and a woman is one of war. I never had any wish to win or to lose, for in winning one loses, in losing one wins. In the long fight both of us won and both lost. It has been said that of Homer's own epics, the *Iliad* is the woman's story—life is a battle; the man's is the *Odyssey* —life is a journey. I have always hated battle, and I was forced into it. Women have least to gain by war, but it is they, at least in part, who start the wars.

Very well. I was on my own. I would fight out the battle for Celia entirely on my own. Of the 'short list' Celia seemed to be the most available. One day I asked if she was free to come to my room after hours. She said she was sorry but she had to go out with a 'dreary boy friend'. I had seen this man, a middle-aged, greying individual who haunted the office door two or three nights a week, waiting for her. This statement of her connection with him was, I realised later, a challenge. A couple of evenings later Celia was free to come to my room. She sat down near me and I asked lightly:

'How was it with the dreary boy friend?'

She shrugged her shoulders and smiled. 'All right. Same as usual.' She looked very young and innocent.

'He's older than you?'

'Yes. He's not living with his wife.'

'He has children?'

'Yes.'

'Do you mind about the wife and children?'

She made a motion almost of impatience. 'Oh, I shouldn't

care about them if I liked him.' Then came the fateful words: 'All I want is that he should be kind, and a gentleman.'

The room, the words, the atmosphere of our meeting were heavy with meaning. I knew she was talking about me, about me and my wife and my children. Her meaning was absolutely clear and the answer was equally clear. I knew she wasn't interested in the 'boy friend', the greying adventurer who used sometimes to take her out after office hours. Her message was simple, unmistakable, demanding one answer only. It is interesting that she should have used those words: 'All I want is that he should be kind, and a gentleman.' Celia was an only child: her mother was a village teacher, kind enough but without much to give; her father was very limited, some kind of petty functionary in the West Country. She had said exactly what I wanted to hear. She didn't care about convention—about the existence of my wife and children. She wished no more than that her first lover should be 'kind, and a gentleman'.

At these words I knew instinctively what to do. I put out my hand, took hers firmly and held it. I had never touched her before. Then, in words I didn't recognise as mine, I said:

'Stand up.'

'No,' she said, 'oh no.'

I didn't stop then to wonder what she meant. I supposed she was trying to ward off my approach. She told me later that it was sheer incredulity: she couldn't believe that I had received and responded so immediately to the unspoken message.

We both got to our feet, and I drew her to me, put my arms round her and kissed her mouth. One often, or perhaps always, embraces a woman for the first time as if it were the conclusion to a long process, like the end of a romantic novel. (Actually it is only the beginning of a relationship, and therefore short and shy.) We were both so surprised at our own audacity that we didn't stay together for long; it was as if we wanted only to get away from each other. After a few moments I said: 'I have to go out tomorrow. Can you come the day after?' She nodded in a matter-of-fact way, and we parted.

Whatever cynicism the following events may have brought, we were both at that time intensely serious and passionate people, capable of infinite suffering and prepared to endure anything. I had been the lover of only one woman all my forty years, and I was unfulfilled. Celia had been passionate and serious all her twenty years, and was a virgin. She rejected the prudential approach of the women's magazines and was prepared for complete surrender without reservation to the first man she chose. Our choice of each other was instantaneous and mutual; there was no question of either persuading the other. If either had been less than whole-hearted, there would have been the end of it. We knew, both of us, that we were in for a bad time, but also that it would be marvellous. Perhaps we both had a streak of masochism, almost as if we relished the hell that we were laying up for ourselves with such calm, unwavering certainty.

My relations with Anne were not such that I could allow her to suspect that I was having an 'affair'. Celia instinctively realised that our relationship must be secret. Accordingly, meetings must be secret too. If anyone in the office knew, then Anne would also know. She knew a good many of my colleagues, and in any case she sometimes came to see me there. So for two months Celia and I met clandestinely, and the secrecy, there is no doubt, added edge and urgency to the relationship. We entered a period of secret meetings, arranged by code. We had no official reason for meeting since Celia was not in my department. But members of the executive, the senior administrators, could leave messages in pigeon-holes reserved for junior members of the firm. So I would often leave a book in Celia's pigeon-hole as I left the office, and at the back of the book would appear a pencilled note: 'Friday 6.15 SR', which indicated that I would meet her the following Friday at 6.15 in the stockroom, where we would come together as if by accident. It worked wonderfully.

I cannot describe these meetings, but any lover can imagine them. I had an instinctive respect for Celia's chastity, which in a young girl is quite as strong, until she had surrendered it, as if she intended to preserve it for ever. I had no wish for physical intimacies which could not be fully consummated —partly because of prudential considerations; partly perhaps because my homosexual side was a restraining influence in my relations with women; partly because I knew we should one day be lovers, and it was more exquisitely erotic to delay the moment of consummation. I was, I realised, an erotic and aesthetic masochist, an artist in passion, rejecting the urgency of youth in favour of the more exquisite delays of maturity. Later, Celia was to reproach me bitterly for my lack of impetuosity. I couldn't help it. Perhaps she was even saying, 'You're getting old.' The truth is, I have never been impetuous. I'm phlegmatic, but perhaps I feel more deeply on that account.

For the time being, however, I thought myself decisive and active enough. For two months we continued in this unresolved, clandestine way. Our courtship was thrilling because we both wanted it equally. Neither had to urge, or to play the coquette; we loved one another instantly and, it seemed, for ever. We never quarrelled. She obeyed my coded instructions to the letter. Our meetings were always delicious, always too short. She never once failed me, nor I her. We kissed, we fondled. We talked idly of ourselves, our associates, our hopes and plans. The time passed easily. We were in no hurry to alter things, and indeed office routine made that impossible.

These two months were for me a peculiarly poignant and intense period. I was for the first time betraying the wife I loved. That gave me no satisfaction. I was also endangering the happiness of the children I adored. That was no cause for complacency. I gambled on everything turning out all right. Whatever happened with Celia, I had no intention of disrupting my domestic life and that of those I loved. It seemed that Celia accepted this. She recognised that she was an interloper without rights and she made no demands. She was, as it were, my slave. She came when I told her to. She was always sweet and unruffled, apparently happy in my love and admiration. As for me, it was transcendentally delicious to feel myself, for the first time in my forty years, wanted for myself alone, for my body, my mind, and all that was me, without any consideration of what I could give in return. I could give Celia nothing but my admiration and love. I could give her no security, no tangible reward—only a clandestine intrigue with a happily married man twice her age. I felt that every man, however regular his life, however emotionally deprived, was entitled to one such relationship. Her absolute desire for me was enormously comforting, flattering and satisfying. I have said that these two months of intensity and delight were an exquisite interregnum. Nothing had been lost, sacrificed : no one was unhappy. No irrevocable decisions had been made. It was like the calm of mobilisation before an inevitable conflict, the Indian summer before an autumn of storm, I could love everyone, without having to make decisions which would affect the future of all of us. My wife suspected nothing : she didn't have a suspicious nature, and in any case we had been married for fifteen years without there having been any cause for jealousy.

One day it happened that Celia and I were obliged to go to some meeting or conference in each other's company. We travelled openly; my wife knew about it. It was all above board. As we sat in a café together, Celia said :

'Isn't it wonderful to be able to meet openly, not to have to pretend !'

She genuinely hated the secrecy. Perhaps I, more devious and reserved than I care to be, enjoyed the atmosphere of conspiracy more than she did. Perhaps she wished I was the kind of man who would go to my wife openly and say, 'I am in love with someone else. Give me my freedom and let me go.'

But she didn't behave as if she wanted me to be more impulsive than it was my nature to be. She passively accepted the need for secrecy, her own rôle as an outsider. It was as if she were waiting fatalistically for chance to give her a different part.

Celia seemed to me each time I saw her more beautiful, more passive and giving, more worthy of the efforts and sacrifices that lead to sheer tragedy. Yet our meetings were always gay. We knew each other's minds, we shared jokes, we shared the hazards of the game of secrecy which we played so expertly. If only someone had told her to get out while she could, if only someone could have urged on me the necessity to make the supreme renunciation. But life is not a romantic novel. Whatever it was we had started, we had to finish it.

One evening we lingered together in a part of the building separated from the corridor by a ground glass partition—we embraced, fondled and parted. But next time we met Celia was in a state of great agitation—her fellow secretaries had seen us silhouetted against the ground glass. Her colleagues ragged her, telling her they had watched while we faced one another, approached and then, as they put it, 'merged'. I told her not to worry: they were merely jealous. She laughed. Nothing mattered.

I gave Celia small presents—a Victorian handbag, mother-of-pearl opera glasses—things she might have and look at and use without being compromised. We didn't talk much about sex; it was unnecessary, since we were living it.

One day she said to me, 'In what way do you love me?' Deliberately, yet without hesitation, as if my words had been dictated by something outside me, I answered: 'With heart—and mind—and body.' My answer satisfied her.

Another day, when we were sitting close to one another but without touching, she asked: 'What do you want to do?' Again I answered, as if I had learned a part: 'To kiss you all over with no clothes on.'

This was simply playing with sex. It was to me as if the words were more important than the act, the declaration than the thing itself. Yet I meant it. To both of us, virgin in a sense as we were, it meant much.

I have been anticipating. The two months I refer to were the months between our first coming together and our first going to bed together. The crucial meeting, which decided our fate, took place a bare week after our first embrace.

We spent a day alone together in the country, far from the office. I invented an excuse for going into the country one

Saturday and Celia was spending that weekend at home in the West Country. We agreed to meet at a little country station convenient to us both. I arrived first, in a fever of impatience to see her. She arrived punctually by bus, and together we set off. The day was perfect—it seemed a good omen. I had brought food for a picnic. We said nothing as we walked away from the station. It was Celia's first secret assignation, mine too. There might be other people in the neighbourhood who would recognise her or me; we wanted to avoid that. As it happened, we saw no one. I had lied to my wife about some essential meeting with a client. I didn't like that, but it had to be done. Celia had more nearly told the truth to her mother and father. Her father had given her a pink rose as she left the house. I doubt whether he had any qualms about the situation. This man had more influence on her than I realised. He was, so to speak, on her side against me. She once, and once only, brought her father and me together. He said next to nothing and couldn't manage to look me in the eye. He was a simple countryman, dignified and inarticulate. I felt towards him as the cad in the Victorian novel would feel towards the father of the girl he intended to ruin, or had ruined.

Within half a mile of the station Celia and I found a deserted field, lying green and peaceful in the early summer sun. It might have been designed for our first secret meeting. We found a bank under some blossoming may trees. I spread out my rainproof coat and we lay down immediately, our arms around each other. So great was my need for her that I put my left hand on her knee and, without due hesitation, ran it up her thigh under her skirt. She brushed my hand away impatiently. I was the most inexperienced seducer imaginable. It didn't matter though. Nothing mattered except that we were together and alone, away from watching eyes and whispering tongues. We stayed there perhaps eight hours before running for our respective train and bus. I have no recollection of what was said between us. We ate our cold food soon after midday. After my first clumsy approach our embraces were warm but not intimate.

'I want to be your lover,' I told her. 'But not now, and not in a field.' She silently assented. The day remained perfect, as did all that summer.

There was no conflict between us then or for long after. Neither of us had any need to win the other. We both accepted the relationship as inevitable, fated. I cannot imagine that it was either of us who started the affair: that is the name by which it has to be called. Each needed the other with his whole being. She had no doubt from the first that she needed me as a lover; I never questioned that she was my predestined and perfect mistress. I had waited many years for her, and she seemed to me perfect. I never knew why I loved her; she was of course beautiful, but so were others. She was young, and so were others. She spoke beautifully, laughed and cried at the same things as I, shared my daily reactions to everything. I didn't realise then that she, like other women in love, had the artistry of total response to her lover's moods and thoughts, the ability to be, exactly and generously, what her lover needed. I don't accuse her of acting; she was herself, then, as always.

We separated and arranged to meet again soon at the office, in a state of mind that cannot be described. For the next two months my whole condition of mind was utterly unlike anything I have experienced before or since. I was in love as I had never been before. True, with my first love, Jane, I had always enjoyed or suffered the same sense of rapt ecstasy, the same intensification of everyday feelings and experience; but now it was with the sensibilities of a mature man who had suffered and lived, who loved others and did not feel himself free, yet was compelled to move gradually into a state of being where tragic consequences become inevitable. At first our relationship existed in a kind of vacuum, or rather in an element different from everyday life, so that the actual world scarcely came into contact with our private world. So long as we were prudent and discreet, patient and unhurried, we could enjoy our love in a totally amoral, irresponsible way: it existed, nothing else did. That was all we knew.

We met when we could, arranged secret rendezvous, talked of anything and everything, laughed, were happy to be seen publicly together on any legitimate occasion, courted chastely, as if in no hurry to anticipate what, in its due time and place, was to be transcendent. We didn't talk about our future—it was simply understood that I would arrange matters when the situation allowed.

My conscience always tormented me when I thought about the wider implications of the affair. Yet I never at this period contemplated exchanging my wife for Celia or deserting my children. Anne and the children made different demands on my love, each was attached to my heart by a thousand small links and threads. I had no thought of detaching them yet I didn't think of the affair with Celia as either trivial or transitory. Neither she nor I was the person to have casual romances. Everything was important, especially in that atmosphere.

It was as if I breathed something other than air, something which, as some drugs are reputed to do, heightened consciousness, but without allaying worry and anxiety. I was myself in every respect, but more intensely so. The beauty of the summer, the pathos of human love, with its divisions, deceptions and contradictions, were present day and night throughout that time. Celia was never out of my thoughts. When I could not see her, I spent the time finding her small presents or love-gifts which would beguile her. I don't know whether she was the perfection of a mistress: I only know that she seemed so, that she made herself so. She was also perfectly modest and well conducted in the way that I would be bound to approve: she never criticised Anne, or showed anything but respect for her. She appreciated my strategies of deception without ever appearing to think them more than a regrettable necessity.

Despite the sense of fate which overhung us, despite all the irreconcilables we were challenging, our meetings were on the whole gay ones. Her beauty, always remarkable, and remarked by strangers, was heightened by her love for me. As for me, although I was conscious of countenancing a great wrong, I knew that I was helpless. I felt that if I made the great renunciation that circumstances demanded, I would be letting down both Celia and myself. I had never had that total and committed love affair that every man knows he is entitled to, once at least in a lifetime. So intense, inevitable and in its way 'right' was the affair with Celia that I instinctively knew it was now or never. If I renounced her, the darkness of death would one day close over me without my having had this supreme experience. This may have been a kind of greed. There is a sense in which the romantic puritan is greedier than the promiscuous philanderer. I had been to bed with only one woman in my life; most of my friends, I knew, had slept with more. I felt, rightly or wrongly, deprived. At the time when the miserable affair with Denise was ending, I had felt a sense of total despair, of utter futility, of emotional and sexual starvation, such as I had never felt before, even in the extremest aridity of spirit. Celia had erupted out of nowhere, out of utter despair, out of the negation of life, like a green and living spear showing above the withered and frozen ground of winter. It would have needed a superhuman effort to forego such an experience.

Celia herself felt obscurely that I looked upon the affair as 'an experience'. In her way she rebuked me for this. Perhaps it was inevitable. I was a married man with responsibilities I had never taken lightly. But she was a young girl to whom love was experience, life itself. She saw me as a family man with a life of his own. She had nothing then, nothing but our love. She felt, whether she would own it or not, an intruder, an interloper. For the time being, however, such thoughts were a cloud no bigger than a man's hand.

Ironically, Anne would rather have been married to a philanderer, so long as he didn't endanger her security, than to a puritan romantic idealist. But this was not in my nature and the situation inevitably grew worse. For the time being, however, all was outwardly happy, and we enjoyed our pastoral romance without apprehension. I have sometimes wondered what would have happened if I had withdrawn and said, 'That was wonderful. I adore you and always shall. But now we are getting too serious and there will be trouble.' But it was out of the question. To begin with, I, and Celia too, were serious from the beginning. We had started nothing lightly. In the second place, we must have known that there would be trouble, and the inevitability of the trouble made our present innocent state all the sweeter and more poignant. It was as if Adam and Eve had foreknown the Fall. We were both committed romantics bound for disaster.

9

I come now to the account I must give of the culmination and climax of my sexual life. Celia and I were by now plighted lovers. She went home in June that year, with an understanding that she would come and stay with me in London the next month. I telephoned her in the West Country by prearrangement about twice a week. She had no telephone at home, and I was obliged to ring her up at the post office, where there was a call-box. Difficult as it was to escape from my home at the appointed time, we never missed our telephone assignations. This was a strange month, me thinking passionately about her every day of my life and counting the days till we should come together. Although the secretive and conspiratorial atmosphere heightened my pleasure and anticipation, giving it the spice of forbidden fruit, I never once relished the necessity to deceive my wife. I felt at once doomed and exhilarated. I was bent on a course from which nothing could deflect me, a course which must end in some kind of disaster.

The weather was unusually serene, warm and sunny. It had been so since our first meeting alone in the meadow. I had met her in another meadow before she had gone home, and we had walked through the fields of glowing buttercups, the pollen thick on our shoes. We were contented in each other's company. There was not to be, nor was there ever, any undue haste in our courtship. It was pursued with the deliberation of a ritual. It was to be her first, perhaps her only, initiation into love. It was to be for me the reward of frustration and abstinence, something for which I had been waiting all my life. It was as if my marriage and the birth of my children were simply an episode on the way. We felt, like other lovers, as if we had been intended for one another from time immemorial. We felt as if our paths, hitherto so far apart, had been mapped by destiny to cross each other exactly at this point in time and space.

We were unspeakably happy. What we talked of on the telephone I cannot recall. I wrote letters, but what I wrote I have forgotten; I don't know if the letters still exist.

Slowly the weeks passed. At last it was arranged that she was to tell her parents of a visit she was to make to a woman friend in London. I told Anne of a business trip I must make, lasting a week and starting on July 17. It was a Monday. I took the train to London and installed myself in a tiny house in Chelsea lent me by a friend who asked no questions. The house was small, the immediate neighbourhood unfashionable. I laid in some food and tried to buy some red roses. I had to content myself with carnations. The scene was set. I unpacked my things in the small sunny bedsitting-room and awaited her ring at the door. Celia was to catch the train to Paddington from the west and take a taxi to the house.

She arrived punctually at about two o'clock. She may have been five minutes or so later than the arranged time, and during those minutes I paced the room and wondered if anything would go wrong. But at last she came. I hadn't seen her for about five weeks. I remember it clearly, and when she came she seemed more radiant, more intense and serious than ever. Her reappearance after these weeks came almost as a shock. If I had had any doubts, they vanished within seconds. She was in my arms. We said little. There was nothing to keep us apart. We had the place to ourselves. The room was warm and flooded with sunlight. The rundown neighbourhood was quiet. No one knew we were there. We were on an island with no one to think of but ourselves.

Celia opened her suitcase and unpacked a few things, including some food she had brought, which was put in the kitchen at the back of the house. We were on the first floor. Curtains protected us from any prying eyes opposite, but they were thin and didn't keep out either the light or the sun.

I pulled down the bedclothes and laid out a towel. Celia was a virgin, and I had no wish that my host's sheets should be stained. I had taken no contraceptive precautions, though I had no intention that Celia should be impregnated. How I was to avoid this contingency I did not know. I had brought some French letters, but I had never used such things with success, and they had always proved unusable with Anne. I had relied on Anne, when we didn't want to have a baby, to use contraceptives, and this she had done with success. But Celia was a virgin, and I didn't think that anything was necessary. To begin with, at any rate, I proposed to trust to luck.

We both wanted each other inordinately. I turned from her and stood with my back to the bed, facing a chair on which I dropped my clothes. I knew that it was necessary for me to be naked first, in order to give her confidence and overcome her shame at being naked in the presence of one who was, after all, a stranger. Neither of us had much on, as the weather was warm. I put my jacket over the back of the chair, then pulled off my shirt. Before I dropped my trousers and laid them on a chair, I first got rid of my socks and shoes, since I realised that a man in these alone might look faintly ridiculous. I felt as if I were performing a sacrificial act, denuding myself for some kind of religious ceremony.

I turned and faced the bed. Celia was already almost naked. She sat on the end of the bed, her back towards me, bowed and submissive. She still had on a girdle round her buttocks and a brassière. From the back, as she sat pressing down the bedclothes slightly, she looked completely naked. I have never forgotten that first sight of her body. The image of it was exactly as it has remained with me ever since. Her short, auburn hair surmounted a soft, rounded neck, and from there her backbone curved expressively downwards until, at its base, it was hidden by her girdle and the bedclothes. It was, literally, the most beautiful thing I had ever seen. Her beauty was heightened by the knowledge that it was wholly mine, to do what I wished with. This back, rounded forwards to her swelling, sloping shoulders and her breasts, hidden by her body and by the brassière, was to me like a newly discovered island to the eyes of a weatherbeaten mariner. Here was all beauty and all pleasure. The combination of hardness of outline with softness of surface was inexpressibly perfect. I believed till then, as I still believe, that of all substances in the world young flesh is the most beautiful, the most desirable. It has not its equal, though makers of cloth have tried in vain for hundreds of years to surpass it. But no satin, silk or damask could equal Celia's skin as it was then, warm and glowing with desire in the afternoon sun of July.

I sat on the bed behind her and put my arms round her. The feel of her naked flesh was indescribably sweet. There was no blemish on her skin. She had in fact spent many hours during the past month sun-bathing on a West Country beach, almost as if she had thought of nothing but to beautify herself for my pleasure. Her flesh was a rich golden brown—she had a naturally fair skin, and it had browned without sallowness and without going red.

From behind her I undid the clasp of the brassière and took it off. Then I turned her towards me, and we both stood up. Next I pulled down the elastic girdle, which was like a sheath over her full loins. We stood naked for the first time in each other's arms, our bodies pressed close all the way from the breast to the knees. Then we lay together on the bed, and I pulled up the clothes over us.

I told Celia later that she had the upper half of a queen and the lower half of a peasant. Despite her essential gracefulness and the beauty with which she moved, she was heavily built. Her shoulders sloped like those of a kangaroo or a Victorian beauty. Her arms were round and full, her hands small and delicate. She took exquisite care of her body, from her hair to her feet. She used powder, but little scent and only a minimum of make-up. Her breasts were not especially beautiful in themselves; her nipples were too far from the centre for classical perfection, and they hung rather than rose. But they were full, not small, maternal rather than anything else. Her belly was smooth and flat, her buttocks round and firm. But what made her in some ways abnormal was the great thickness and strength of her thighs and the consequent difficulty of access to her vagina. I always found it difficult and uncomfortable to fuck her unless her knees were pressed upwards as far as possible in the direction of her shoulders. In this position her vagina was easily accessible to me; but of course like this she became stiff, and we were obliged to change our position to something nearer the normal.

We lay there for many hours. At last, tired and almost drunk with sexual pleasure, we dressed and got some food. We spent most of the next few days in bed. Fucking made us enormously hungry. We ate a lot and always felt in the perfection of health. It took me at least two days to take Celia's virginity. Her membrane was immensely strong and impenetrable. I tried to be gentle, but it was not the way. After two days my friend Simon, who was in our confidence, came to call. He had more experience than I, and when I told him of my difficulties, he said that it was sometimes necessary to be violent. He also upbraided me strongly for taking no contraceptive precautions and went out to buy me the most up-to-date efficacious ones from the nearest chemist.

At last Celia and I became lovers in the completest sense, and I tired myself out daily in satisfying her. She had, certainly, an inordinate sexual appetite, once it was roused. She took all she could get. Her greed was natural, unthinking, and it delighted me to satisfy it. All the same I think that a younger man would have given more. I have heard of young men in their early twenties fucking a woman up to twelve times in one night, but I believe the most I achieved was five, and that was in reality more than I wanted. But I was obsessed with the idea of satisfying Celia, of sacrificing myself to her needs. In giving her pleasure I satisfied myself. I was, I think, imbued with the notion of self-immolation. It was as if I worshipped her body and wished no other fate than to die in giving her pleasure. The metaphore of sexual death by orgasm is known to everyone who has had complete sexual fulfilment. There was one feeling which superseded all others in my mind during that week—even the feeling of joy, fulfilment, supreme happiness; and that was the sense of death. It was as if some part of me were dying, or as if I were wholly dying. More than once I told myself that at any moment during that week I would gladly have died. This was no metaphor; I meant it. I learned from that moment that the obstinate love of life is the expression of unhappiness. I was completely happy in the service of Celia's love and lust. I had achieved what had been denied me until the age of forty, and I knew that no later happiness would ever equal this. Why then go on living? To live fully is to experience at least one supreme hour when one does not care if one goes on living or not.

I was, I suppose, to some extent living a part. I made a profession of doing all I did to serve Celia. At this stage she was comparatively undemanding. It was later that her lust for me became almost too much. The sexual experience I had with her was very different from that which I had had with Anne. Here I was the master, the man of experience. I felt my body full of strength, energy and ruthless drive. I fucked aggressively and masterfully. This was partly because, being no longer in my first youth, I could restrain the moment of climax and give my partner the joy of a long-delayed orgasm. I was very active, Celia very passive. She scarcely made a sound. I, on the other hand, talked incessantly, saying whatever came into my head about Celia's beauty or my lust. 'I want to stab you,' I would say, 'and stab—and stab—and stab—and stab—and stab' in the rhythm of my action. I then understood, through this compulsive articulation of my feelings, why aggressive action is so often sexual, and why sexual criminals feel a compulsion to stab their victims. I did not bite Celia very much as I couldn't bear to mark her skin, but I kissed her mouth incessantly until she developed a rash from the rasping of my shaven chin and had to apply some healing cream. She was always silent and undemonstrative, not gasping or singing or vocalising her pleasure in any way. I was never quite sure of the moment when she had an orgasm. I believe it was continuous. She was passive so long as I fucked, never protested when at last I had to stop, and never pressed for more than I could give. She was, at this time at any rate, a perfect mistress. I adored her, and the experience was so transcendent, so absolute, that I could conceive of no other existence. I would willingly have died in Celia's arms.

The ecstasy of unreality continued. We loved blindly on through the week. We ate mostly at home—Celia was an excellent provider. We would go shopping together and walk out in the streets in the cool of the evening. We were never separated. We bathed together and washed each other's bodies in loving tenderness. It seemed I had something I could cherish and care for, as my own body, now trembling alive as if it had cast off years of shrivelled greyness, was loved and cared for. We felt also a sense of doom, but we didn't discuss the inevitable strains and heartbreak that must some time follow. We did not show our love in public. For one thing, there were people in the neighbourhood who might know me. One night, as we were walking, Celia said softly, 'Kiss me, there's no one in sight.' We never kissed in full view of others, even when we were in a district where no one could know us. Occasionally in a public street we held hands, but almost furtively. All the time my sense of utter dreamlike happiness continued, combined with a sense of the desirability of death. 'If it were now to die, 'twere now to be most happy.' I understood the words of Othello at the first and last moment of his complete happiness.

During that week we didn't indulge in any unconventional caresses. The discovery of a lover's body is a long process, the longer the better. So is the discovery of the many varied pleasures of physical intimacy. These I had never discovered with my wife, if only because there was always a certain shyness between us. I take the blame for this, and attribute it to my intensely puritan and frustrated upbringing. Nowadays young people can learn a great deal about sex from novels openly available. It was more difficult when I was first married. The sex books were not very helpful, and fiction dealt in evasions and suppressions. One thing I learned for myself. I had never fucked Anne except in the dark, apart from a very few early morning occasions. I never fucked Celia except with the light on, and it gave me exquisite pleasure to watch the changing expressions on her beautiful face with its shut eyes and half-open lips.

The next week began to draw to an end. On the last day but one Celia became withdrawn and thoughtful. In the afternoon my friend Simon visited us for the second time. Celia seemed very anxious to talk to him alone. They went into the next room, and I heard them talking in undertones—I couldn't catch their drift. Simon left and the next morning we began disconsolately to pack and clear up. I went out of the room for something, and when I returned, Celia was lying on the bed, not crying but in a state of distress. She confessed that she was wishing that a certain thing would happen. Not wanting to ask her directly, I asked: 'Does it involve anyone's death?' I meant, of course, had she allowed herself to wish my wife would die and leave us free to marry? Celia smiled the ghost of a smile and said no. She could not, of course, have wished anything so dramatic and simple. Then she said, 'What would *any* girl wish?'

Slowly her meaning got through to me. I was inwardly appalled, for it had not so far for a single moment occurred to me that I could possibly leave Anne. I forgot what I said, but I gave her no reason to hope. In actual fact, though she perhaps didn't realise it, she was planting temptation in my mind. A little later she began to cry. I took her in my arms. She was almost angry. In a tone of bitter reproach she said, 'I've been living for a whole week with a man who doesn't love me.'

The words were like a dagger. I denied her accusation, but I could not forget either it or the tone of her utter devastation, the crumpled huddle of her defeated body in my arms.

What is sincerity? She meant what she said, but her action, almost her act, was deliberate and studied. Women have a capacity for showing what they mean which is almost unknown to men, except perhaps to some types of actor. I learned later that she had asked Simon the day before whether she should try to keep me, to get me away from Anne. Although he blamed himself for this afterwards, he could not in the circumstances have done otherwise than advise her to go ahead. He knew of my unhappiness with Anne and my happiness with Celia. He could no more foresee the consequences of his advice than he could have foretold the effect on me if he had advised otherwise. Whether Celia would have done as she did and deliberately made a bid for me had not Simon given her this advice, no one can tell. He was himself young, a little older than Celia herself, and I think he was in a way on her side, as he certainly was on mine. In any case I thought of Celia's desolation and of the awfulness of her plight every day and night until I saw her again.

From then on, had I known it, our relationship was in her hands—it would go as she willed. We said no more on the matter, and she cheered up. We said good-bye to each other at Paddington, and the misery of our parting was mutual.

I rang her up at home during the following week, as before. She seemed contented with things as they were. We had arranged to have two nights together in London the following weekend. The house where we had been was not available. I was obliged to find a hotel, a thing I had never done before in such circumstances. The small hotels near Paddington were seedy and disreputable. The last thing a man in my situation wants to do is to make his mistress feel like a whore. I found the one hotel in a long row of them which appeared, and indeed claimed to be 'respectable'. I said I wanted a quiet room for myself and my wife for two nights, bed and breakfast, and signed the register as for myself and my wife. This gave an added sense of guilt which I didn't relish.

Celia caught the afternoon train and when she arrived we went straight upstairs. I undressed her and made her lie on her back along the bottom of the double bed. Then I knelt down and kissed her whole body from her knees to her lips. I too was naked. But she was impatient, with a compulsive physical impatience I was to get to know. She said, 'I don't want to be kissed, I want to be fucked.' She had wanted me incessantly the whole week. I too was full of lust, strengthened and refreshed by a week's abstinence. Her vagina was larger, more open and more lubricated than before. I arranged the towel under our bodies and pushed the two jelly-like pellets as far into Celia as I could. Soon I had penetrated her and was fucking, slowly, almost calculatingly, wishing to give her the very maximum pleasure of which she was capable. It was still daylight, and I delighted to watch her half-shut eyes with an almost cruel tenderness as I played on her insatiable and responsive body. It was like a ritual or a dance with rules and rhythm of its own. It was the most perfect sex experience of my life—and I remember very little of it except its length and its perfection. As I began to move in and out of her body I noticed my left hand lying, palm downwards beside her face. My watch showed me the time. I moved rhythmically, sometimes faster, sometimes more slowly, and since her vagina exerted no grip, I felt as if I could have gone on for ever and not reached a climax. At last I had to stop, so I hastened my climax and reached the state of panting and groaning that precedes release. At the right moment I took my handkerchief from under the pillow, withdrew my penis and ejaculated into it. I looked at my watch. We had been fucking for an hour and ten minutes without stopping. I slept in utter oblivion for an hour or so. Afterwards we washed and dressed and went out to a restaurant for dinner. We were very hungry.

Men with whom I have discussed it are divided about coitus interruptus. On the whole, the young men do not like it; older men do. When one is older, one is more cautious. But there is more to it than that. In his maturity a man with a young mistress desires only to give her the maximum pleasure, perhaps at the minimum risk. The climax inside her is less important than that she should have all the pleasure she can get. In Celia's pleasure was my happiness. As a lover I spoiled her, but that was what I wanted.

10

Celia went back to the country again. Her job with my firm was now on a less regular basis than before. Her mother's health was bad, and she was obliged to spend much time at home. We communicated by letter and telephone. Now began a series of long, passionate letters. She told me on the last occasion I have described that she was expecting the curse the following week. It was late, and she was worried. She consulted a nursing friend of hers and then sent her mother out for the day to an aunt and passed a long time in a mustard bath. This had the result she wanted, and all was well. She never became pregnant through me.

With Anne life went on outwardly the same. After I had become Celia's lover I found I could no more fuck my wife. She said nothing—we had always been reticent about our sexual relations—but she must have felt my withdrawal from her. The affair with Celia was no mere affair. I had no idea how it could end. Perhaps I thought it would continue on this basis indefinitely. I was deeply in love, as I have never been before or since, and Celia was at this time equally in love with me. When she was working with the firm she often came to my room where we sometimes made love. One day she was late, having been out with a young man. She was contrite and apologetic, but I'm sure she had the subconscious idea of testing me. She quoted someone as saying, 'Where there is no jealousy, there is no love.' She told me later that I ought to have put her across my knees and beaten her. She was very young and had been brought up in an old-fashioned way in the country. I had no desire to beat her then—that came later.

When she was away I thought of her continually, during

every waking moment. I told her in one letter that the image of her young, full, naked body went before me like a rosy cloud. The sort of thing I told her in letters has, in retrospect, the ring of pornography and I suppose one's private thoughts about sex are always commonplace, even vulgar—vulgar at any rate when they are written down. But to write was a compulsion. I poured out in my letters all the dammed-up lust and longing that had built up during the past ten years and more. I described in detail how we had made love, and how I hoped to make love in the future. 'We are standing together,' I would write, 'naked, face to face. I put my arms round you, stroke your bottom and kiss your breasts. I cannot resist you. I draw you to the bed and we lie there together', and so on. Celia liked these letters. They were the next best thing to our being together. Her own letters were never long and erotic. She expressed passion with her body, not in words. She had a profound sense of shame, which it was part of my pleasure to outrage, and part of her pleasure to have outraged for my sake. With other people, with very occasional exceptions, she was cool and offhand. She would have passed for a very cool and self-possessed person. Every lover must want to have his mistress so. I wrote to her and sent her small presents, things she had mentioned that she wanted—antique rings, an ivory fan, prettily Edwardian. I took pleasure in finding things she would like; she had excellent taste. We had much in common, quite apart from our delight in each other's bodies. We enjoyed music, painting, plays, and particularly we enjoyed the same private jokes about other people. She had an enormous sense of fun when she was with me. Love irradiated her whole personality, she was gay and carefree. Approaching destiny was only a passing cloud.

We slept together a number of times before Christmas, when the crisis came which I will come to soon. It was usually for two nights at the weekend. I found that the best way to get accommodation was simply to meet Celia at Paddington and tell the taxi-driver that my wife and I needed a quiet, respectable hotel. They always knew the right ones, and after the first couple of times I got over my embarrassment at making a stranger an accomplice in one's guilt. I always entered us in the register as man and wife under my own name. On one occasion at breakfast the waiter spoke of Celia as my 'daughter'. We laughed over this and made a joke of it. After this Celia would sometimes refer to me as her grandfather: 'Surely a nice girl can go out with her grandfather without people staring at her.' One hotel was rather squalid; I found a used French letter thrown on top of the wardrobe. In another hotel a waiter looked at us so suspiciously that Celia didn't like it and said we should not go there again. On arriving at a discreetly respectable hotel near Baker Street, the taximan was tipped half a crown by the proprietor, who slipped the coin into his hand as she showed us up the steps. It was obviously prearranged. I suppose hotel managers are accustomed to get trade in this way, and I imagine they are pretty firm with the taximen as to what kind of clients they bring. It was, I thought, to Celia's and my credit that we were usually taken to quiet, respectable, even old-fashioned places.

After the summer holiday Celia and I continued to meet as often as we could, secretly. This was not very often in fact. The infrequency and the secrecy of our meetings heightened the intensity of our feelings. We got into a situation from which neither of us could conceive of withdrawing; the strain was terrible but thrilling. I thought almost continuously of Celia—her body, her voice, her face were an obsession. I continued to give her presents, spending much time when she was away planning what I could give her that would most please her. Nothing I gave her was very expensive; I was not then well enough off to give expensive presents. But all were chosen with loving care and appreciated as such. Celia was a recipient worth giving to; her gratitude and delight were always spontaneous and unreserved. She loved things which most young people would think old-fashioned.

Ours was a living, growing love, and no such relationship can remain static. That which at first had been unthinkable now became possible—this was my separation from my wife and, I imagined, my children, since Anne would certainly not wish to part with them. What was possible became feasible, indeed compulsory. Still I told Celia I would never leave Anne. She would have to tell me to go.

One day we were having tea in a café near Paddington; we were weekending in London at some small quiet hotel. Celia said, 'What do you plan to do?' I said, 'I shall tell Anne. Then it is up to her.' Celia agreed. My conscience, already oppressed with guilt, told me I was, predictably, throwing all the burden of decision on another. I would act dishonourably, but it would not be I who made the decision. I would force Anne to make it. In this, as it chanced, I was wrong. There were many things about Anne I did not understand—indeed, many things about women.

Over the Christmas holiday Celia went for some days to her home in the country. We spoke to each other by telephone. Then she came up to London, and we agreed to stay together. I told Anne I was going to my mother's house for a few days. Celia and I had our usual weekend—inexpensive restaurants, a theatre, a concert, and our nights together—sexually and in emotional companionship always the most perfect part of our times together. I had, my conscience told me, made my mistakes as a lover with Anne, and Celia was now reaping the reward. My rule for happiness was always to aim for Celia's pleasure. In the long run, I now realise, this would not have worked, for it would lead to demands I could not satisfy; Celia was my junior by twenty years. But for the time being all was perfect. At other times Celia practised a kind of small-scale guerrilla sex war. She knew I took her occasional contrariness too seriously. By nature I am peaceable and basically cowardly, so I gave in to her. This was the seed of that dominance she would have achieved over me if we had ever lived together permanently. The one who is stronger sexually is the dominant partner.

A friend had told Celia of a certain restaurant, a small, cheap one in Soho. I agreed we should look for it. We were hungry and it was late. Up and down those poky streets we searched. At last, towards two o'clock, we found it. It looked unappetising, but we went in. I was by now fuming inwardly, but Celia could rarely make me outwardly angry. Afterwards I relented, and Celia became friendly and considerate. 'Well,' she said, 'we did find it.' 'Still, you must admit the food wasn't too good,' I replied. 'Oh, ghastly!' she agreed gaily, conceding all I could have wanted. The trivial incident was over. I was, in a way, still getting to know Celia, and it fascinated me.

Before our usual tearful, lingering farewell I told Celia I would tell Anne about us when I got home. I felt we were being driven by some Hardyesque destiny on a course whose end we could not foresee and which was bound to end in unhappiness for one, and perhaps for three people. Nothing, I was determined, would make me give up Celia voluntarily. There was no help for it.

When I got home I found that Anne's widowed mother was staying with us. After supper we sat round the fire, talking of ordinary things. It seemed as if she would never go off to bed, though she usually went quite early. At last she said goodnight and left Anne and me alone together.

'I thought she'd never go to bed. I have to tell you something,' I began.

It all seemed so inevitable. It came out of almost any middlebrow domestic novel, and yet it was happening to us.

'I haven't been to my mother's house,' I went on. 'I've been staying in London with a girl.'

Anne looked up. She must have been thinking quickly.

'Celia,' she guessed.

I nodded. Anne had seen us together. Perhaps she suspected something, but she never showed her suspicions. Feminine instinct at a time when domestic security is threatened is well known, but its sureness and swiftness cannot be credited until they have been experienced at first hand.

Anne didn't know what to think or say. The details of the ensuing scene I have forgotten. I remember only her mingled accusations and reproaches, her tears of sincere distress that this was my first deviation, actual or suspected, and that our friends had always held me up as a model husband, whatever my faults in some directions. To be a good husband was the task I had accepted when fifteen years before I realised, after a week of marriage, that I had made a great mistake. Now at last I had made up my mind that I had atoned for this mistake and that I could live with it no longer.

Anne accused me of revenging myself for love affairs she had had before she met me. 'No,' I told her, 'I have never held those against you. How could I?'

But perhaps unconsciously I had. Perhaps I grudged her the formative experiences my own nature had denied me. I am now convinced that no marriage should take place between two people who have not each 'made their mistakes'. The fact that I was a virgin when I married was part of my fatal romanticism, pride or vanity, or whatever it was. Now time was taking its revenge on me and my wife. She alone had been innocent. In fifteen years our incompatibility, as I saw it, had built up into an impassable barrier. She was very near the tragic age, for a woman, of forty. I was at that, for a man, triumphant and decisive age. All men should marry at forty, and none before. Those who have read so far will understand me well enough to know that I suffered all Anne's anguish during the succeeding months. There *is* such a thing as happy love, but love is not in itself happy.

My affair with Celia lasted for just over another year. It was a year of agony and tension; every now and again I would report to Celia by telephone that Anne and I had had another emotional bloodbath. She was truly sympathetic; she knew what I must be enduring for her sake—our sake. I told Anne I now realised we had never really been compatible and that I was deeply sorry for her sake that I had not made this known earlier. 'Why did you tell me about Celia?' she asked angrily. 'I wouldn't have minded your having a secret affair. But now I see it's because you want to leave me. Yes, that's it.'

At first she talked wildly of going to join a cousin of hers in India. At other times she seemed resigned and was broken and tearful. I felt like a vivisectionist. 'It's ghastly,' I said, 'I suppose one only cries for oneself.' 'Or for the children,' she said, more in sadness than in bitterness. I could not bring myself to give up the idea of being with Celia, though half of me wanted to stay with Anne and the children. I too was torn in half.

My relationship with Celia gradually became clouded. On the surface nothing had changed. We still saw one another and went to bed together when we could snatch a weekend. Perhaps what she wanted was not the permanent relationship I thought we both wanted, but simply the excitement, the danger, the novelty of losing her virginity with an older man who loved her. She liked men of my age. She wanted and needed sex. Perhaps too she was flattered to have taken me from another woman. She was quick, instinctive, intensely feminine, a girl of moods who often didn't know her own mind or the direction in which her passions were leading her.

It was soon clear to me that Anne was not going to act the noble and self-sacrificing wife. She went to visit mutual friends of ours and got their advice. I imagine they told her sensibly that if she did nothing it might blow over, I might come to my senses—I could imagine their saying it. What I didn't know, and perhaps they did, was that I was in the grip of a sexual obsession, common to men of my age, and that with it were bound up all sorts of personal inadequacies, failures of my earlier life and experience. I was having with Celia so much of what I had missed when I was Celia's age.

Some scenes were intensely unpleasant. One such I cannot forget. I went away for a weekend with Celia. Naturally I didn't say where I was going, but of course Anne knew. It was Celia's and my custom each to bring a towel—the hotels often didn't provide them. On this occasion we used Celia's, being the larger, to dry ourselves. I laid mine under us on the bed. This was a mistake, for when I got home I foolishly put it in the laundry basket. When Anne took it out the signs of our love-making were obvious. She was scornfully denunciatory, demanding how I could possibly have humiliated her in this way. Sex can be messy.

The year went on. I had to have a mastoid operation early the following spring. Celia once again asked me what I was planning to do and I told her that when I had recovered from the operation I would tell Anne that I must leave her. In the course of one of our weekends early in the autumn she said to me suddenly, 'Just in case anything goes wrong between you and me, I've found a friend.'

I was deeply shocked. I should not have been; she had given me her whole emotional self for nearly a year and a half, and that, as a friend of mine told me afterwards, is a long time in the life of a girl of twenty. She was, perhaps only unconsciously, looking round for a way of escape from a situation in which she was beginning to feel trapped, now that the realities of separation between Anne and me and marriage between Celia and me were looming up to replace the romance and novelty of a secret liaison. She was also, perhaps unconsciously, issuing a warning: 'Hurry, or it will be too late.'

Celia's new friend was a colleague in her new office in north London, and he had lodgings in the same house as her. He was a Welsh youth of about the same age as Celia. He amused her, he was good company; they both liked music and poetry. I met him, since Celia was anxious that we should be on friendly terms. She didn't tell him she was my mistress, as he was very conventional, coming from a chapel-going, hymn-singing home near Swansea. He treated me with respect, but I could form no opinion of him except that he seemed inoffensive and immature. I didn't encourage Celia in arranging these triangular meetings—they were no pleasure to me. Celia forbade me to mention our relationship to Owen. Had I wished to cool his interest in her, I might well have done so. But the choice must be hers. Nevertheless we continued in our plan to go off and live together as soon as I had recovered from my impending operation—to get married if I could get a divorce. Celia loved me and enjoyed going to bed with me, but I think she was falling in love with Owen, who was slim, tall and personable.

I was in a sexually hyperconscious state, caused perhaps by a certain morbidity and heightened excitement arising from the prospect of my operation and my obsession with Celia. During long absences from Celia, I began to take notice of other girls. At certain stages a sexual obsession precludes interest in any other person, at other times it induces a polygamous phase. A girl called Susan, who was extremely attractive, set herself deliberately to conquer me. She did not then succeed, but we kissed and embraced. I used her as a confidante about Celia's and my difficulties over Anne, but I didn't tell Susan of my intentions. She was in reality in desperate need of security and love. Although maddeningly desirable, she didn't want sexual experience—certainly not with me. Another girl, Emma, also came to see me often, and would tell me of her engagement to a very difficult young Irishman. She was deeply sympathetic to me and we too kissed and fondled one another when we could be alone together.

A dull and hopeless resignation possessed Anne and aroused my deepest compassion. I was now set on my course, and nothing could stop me except the unforeseen actions of others. I was of course, in my usual moral cowardice, waiting for someone else to save us all. Unconsciously I wanted to stay with Anne, but I was passionately determined not to lose Celia. One day a few weeks before my operation, Celia and I were talking of Owen and after a long silence she said, sighing deeply: 'Oh, why can't you ever do something on impulse?'

There was tenderness in her reproach. I said nothing. She must take me as I was, or not at all. What she meant was that, if I didn't take this opportunity and run away with her, it might be the last. I had told her, however, quite clearly that I would go away with her after my convalescence and not before.

When the day was decided for me to go into hospital, I

became apprehensive and longed for sympathy. Anne gave it to me as fully as she was able and could not have been kinder or more considerate. Then I asked her if she would mind Celia coming down for the weekend. Magnanimously, she agreed. She didn't have it in her to refuse a sick man anything. The weekend passed off very properly and Anne left Celia and me alone together a good deal of the time. Indeed, she went to bed early, leaving me with Celia to talk and make love in front of the fire. It was, a cynic might say, a good 'move' on Anne's part, for during the weekend the two women drew unconsciously together. There is a sort of women's union in these things, unspoken, without rules. Each saw that neither was a fiend, that neither was evil-intentioned. Women understand more from what is not said than from what is.

During the fortnight I was in hospital after the operation I was in a fever to know what was happening to Celia. As soon as I was well enough I rang her from my private ward. I learned that she was staying with Owen at the house of a cousin of hers in Portsmouth. She told me afterwards that Owen was in love with her and that they had stripped and gone to bed together, but without his losing his virginity. He was very prudish and no doubt scared. She said that she was conscious that her body was not beautiful (she was evidently more critical of it than I, though I could recognise objectively that it was not classically perfect) and that she wanted Owen to see her as she really was. She never, to my knowledge, deceived me in anything, though she was quite capable of innocent deception if it were necessary—of her parents, for instance.

As soon as I was home again, I once more asked Anne if Celia could come for the weekend. She agreed and Celia said she would come. I rested, as far as I could, in feverish impatience, and then Celia rang up to say that she would not come that weekend, but the next. I was in an agony of jealousy and doubt. I was sure she was spending the time with Owen, as indeed she was.

But a morbid fear cannot be quenched except by the truth,

and I shared my secrets with Emma, and asked her what she thought would happen. She said simply: 'I am afraid for you' and no more. She was trying to comfort me in what she guessed would be inevitable disaster.

Celia came down on the Friday evening. When we were alone together, she told me: 'I don't want to go away with you. I don't want to marry you or live with you.'

The axe that beheaded me was very firmly wielded, very deliberately, and not unkindly considering Celia knew what her decision must mean to me. I loved and wanted her more than ever. I would not accept her decision. But what was there to be said; I knew that she had deliberated with herself in great unhappiness for several weeks. What I didn't know, but came later to understand, was that she was using the poor Welsh clerk as a means of escape. She said later that she was in love with him, but it was mere infatuation, there was no depth in her love for him.

We sat together on the sofa, and the fire burned with a cheerful, flickering light, the only light in the room. After some time, when I knew that everything was over between us, Celia began slowly to caress me, nestling closer and closer like a cat making friends. Before long she had so inflamed me that there was only one thing I could do. I went mad and, with the half-conscious idea of making her pregnant and so committing her life to mine, I dragged her to the floor in front of the fire, pulled up her skirt and forced myself into her. Our sexual contact was violent, rapid and complete. I don't think she had foreseen it or known what she was doing. She proclaimed a sense of outrage and turned on me with scorn. 'There,' she said accusingly, 'sex—that's all you ever wanted.' This was so patently absurd and untrue that, even as she said it, Celia didn't believe it. Presently she forgave the outrage and we parted with gentleness and mutual respect.

'I hope I don't have a child,' Celia said. 'If I do, well, you'll have to have me.'

She was in fact two or three days from menstruation, and she did not become pregnant.

The rest of the weekend dragged by in an atmosphere of

incredible unreality. Next morning Celia and I went for a walk. There were no recriminations, only tender solicitude for each other. She told me she would leave next day, Sunday, but that she couldn't go alone. She rang Owen and ordered him to come and take her back home. He turned up that day and she installed him in a hotel; he did exactly as she told him. My last evening with her was spent quietly in her arms. Obviously she had loved me and she still loved me, but it was the twelve-and-a-halfth hour; tomorrow we should part. She caressed me once more, took my erect penis from my trousers and kissed it tenderly. Then we separated for the night. What kind of suspense and uncertainty Anne was in all this time I could not tell.

Next day Owen came to lunch. It was a horrible meal, a gathering of ghosts. But I have forgotten to record that morning. Owen turned up at about ten o'clock from his hotel, and Celia and he and I adjourned to my room, where we talked. Celia told me in his presence that she wished to marry him and wanted me to let her go. I wonder if she was pleading with me to betray her and say the words that would send him packing and commit her to me. 'Owen,' I would say, 'why not get wise to things—Celia has been my mistress for over eighteen months.' But I couldn't bring myself to do this, anguished as I was. I wasn't going to get possession of anyone by such a trick. It would perhaps have been better if I had. He was too innocent—I could have given him the chance to take her as she was, a mature woman with a lover twice her age. As it was, she knelt at my feet and buried her face in my lap, while the Welsh clerk looked on, helpless. 'Let me go,' she moaned, while I stroked her auburn hair. All I could do was to turn to Owen and say (it must have been a surprise to him), 'you fool, you poor blind fool!'

There was nothing more for anyone to say. After the ghost meal they left to catch their train. Before she left, Celia kissed Anne. The women's club had won.

I was in a state of near-hysteria. Anne told me afterwards she had thought I would go with Celia. She was profoundly thankful I had stayed. She was very good to me. Her forgiveness was apparent in tone and gesture, not in words. We never talked of the affair, but it left its lasting mark on our lives.

I will summarise the rest of Celia's story, as far as I know it. She and Owen were married, and a week later she rang up to speak to me.

'Owen and I were married yesterday,' she said ruefully.

I asked her why she had rung up and why she sounded so despondent. She didn't answer.

'You miss me?' I went on, 'and intimacy with me?'

'Yes,' she admitted.

I knew that she meant that Owen had been a washout as a lover on their marriage night. How else could it be; I was a practised lover when I took her virginity, and I had made my mistake with Anne fifteen years earlier. Now Owen had made his mistake with her, and she was disappointed. I felt a certain twisted sense of triumph. I'm not proud of this, I record how I felt.

Owen paid for his mistake with a wrecked marriage. I saw Celia from time to time during the following year or so. After that I lost interest. I am very hard once I've been betrayed, or think I have been betrayed, by someone. Celia gradually became estranged from her husband and allowed herself to be courted by other men. She had always told me that she didn't want children; she was a courtesan rather than a mother and a home-maker. She eventually became pregnant by another man, a married man, and Owen left her and got a divorce. What became of him I never heard. She had a baby boy who was taken into a home, poor little devil. He will now be, I suppose, about sixteen. I don't understand women who bear children and leave them to fend for themselves in this terrible world. The lack of maternal instinct is something I can't understand in any woman, though I am not of course proud of my own part in the business. If we were all conscious of the burdens of our own guilt they would become unbearable.

Although I am a believer in a 'clean break'—unlike most women who, so far as I can see, adhere to the theory of the 'beautiful friendship' once passion has died—I couldn't suddenly let go of the person who had been the object of all my thoughts and desires for nearly two years. I met Celia clandestinely, and we would have rather miserable teas together in the West End. I couldn't bring myself to tell Anne that I was still seeing Celia.

I don't blame Celia for a trivial incident that happened after perhaps a year of this, but it was an incident which—and this is perhaps revealing of my not too admirable nature—finally disillusioned me about her. Never having much money she always, naturally enough, looked to me as the provider. Feeling in my notecase to pay for tea, I inadvertently pulled out a five pound note instead of a one pound note. I put it away and paid for the tea with the one pound note. Celia noticed the fiver. We walked together, arm in arm, up Regent Street. She liked clothes and could never have enough. She stopped at a shop window where hung a nice little short coat priced at ten pounds.

'I love that,' she said. 'If I could borrow five pounds from you, I've got enough to make up the rest myself.'

Out came the fiver. I told her I didn't want to be repaid. A humiliating end to what had started so romantically. No woman can blame Celia for this, but no man can blame me for losing interest in the person who had once meant to me more than happiness itself. Much later Celia tried again to get in touch with me. I ignored her letter. Where she was concerned, rigor mortis had set in.

II

The time that followed Celia's marriage was for me a confused and painful one. I think I had been secretly hoping to start up relations with her again, but nothing came of it. Her attempt to accept me as a mutual friend of her and her husband had failed; I have never been good at three-cornered relationships. Although I had enjoyed great sexual satisfaction on the last occasions when I had been to bed with Celia, these occasions were necessarily too rare to satisfy completely my deep sexual need at this time of my life. I felt as if something had been violently wrenched away from me, as if I had been a starving man who had been allowed to start on a splendid and appetising meal and had had it suddenly snatched away long before the dish was empty. In my sexual starvation I looked round desperately for other satisfactions. I took up sexual relations once more with Anne, but my emotional need for someone young and ardent, as Celia had been, was not fulfilled. I tried desperately to seduce Susan, who was always on the point of giving in but never did. She was what is called a cock-teaser, but I didn't blame her. I wanted it like that, having a strong streak of masochism. I was in any case clumsy and not cut out to be a seducer of women. I have never been to bed with anyone who was initially unwilling. Susan liked to be kissed and caressed to the limit, but no more. It was to me a welcome agony. She was flattered by my interest and attention, but no more.

Emma was another girl whom I would happily have gone to bed with, but I had scruples on account of her engagement to her young Irishman. It didn't seem to me worthy of myself to risk ruining a marriage when I had no intention of forming a permanent relationship with her. I never again had any wish to leave Anne, so that all my other efforts to seek sexual satisfaction with young women were no more than philandering. My youthful unrealistic idealism had failed on my own account but still survived in the hope I had of young virgins. Had I not perhaps caused enough harm to Celia? In a sense I didn't know what it was I wanted. I think I was forcing myself intellectually to compensate for the deprivation of my earlier life. Perhaps my generation and earlier ones have in many ways led unsatisfactory lives through trying to live out too late impulses that were not acted on in childhood and youth. Everything a boy or a young man feels an impulse to do and, because of some inhibition or prohibition, does not do, is liable to be acted out in middle age to the detriment of his proper development. For this reason the so-called permissiveness of contemporary society may make for greater happiness and self-fulfilment, painful though many of its manifestations are. In some ways life was easier for young people when there were external sanctions against certain conduct; the young of today have to make continual choices, which is a hard burden.

During the next few years I interested myself in a number of young women, but my relations with none of them were intimate enough to be worth recording. As it is, I have now, at the age of nearly sixty, slept with only two women. An exception must be made, I had almost forgotten to say, in the case of Emma, my friend and confidante at the time of crisis over Celia. She always was, and still is, fond of me—very fond. Since her marriage I have seen her at irregular intervals, secretly as far as Anne was concerned, openly as far as her husband was concerned. She concealed very little from him. She is devoted to her husband Martin, and would never leave him nor, more than strictly necessary, deceive him. I have offered to meet him, but he has no wish to meet me. He is a sulky, if not sullen, person—somewhat lazy and wrapped up in his own comforts. The basis of Emma's unhappiness is that he has steadfastly refused to allow her to have a child, which she has always passionately wanted. She could have left Martin on grounds of mental cruelty, but she would never do so because he needs her. Sex and reproduction are not uppermost in the minds of some women and Emma is one of them. She has sacrificed her desire for posterity to her motherly affection for Martin. I don't judge this; I simply record it. She also loves me, and we have lain together naked on two occasions, at widely separated intervals. In both cases we were cold and I couldn't achieve coition. I would have given her a baby, whatever the consequences and, latterly, when it became clear that she would never have one by Martin, she would have been glad of this and would have deceived him into thinking it was his. Indeed, she has tried many times to deceive him as to the effectiveness of her contraceptive methods. But she has never conceived a child, and she is now, I think, nearing the age of thirty-seven.

Emma is not, in any obvious sense, beautiful, but she has beauty. Her skin is fresh and clear, her hair blonde and pretty. Her spectacles detract from the obvious attractiveness of her face but her body is very beautiful, and the warmth and ardour of her physical affection are perhaps her chief attractions. She loves physical contact and used to kiss and fondle me in a wholly delightful way—we are very similar in this. As with me, her hands are her most restless sexual organs. We have never quarrelled, and our too infrequent meetings have always been a delight. She is lively and quick of mind, humorous and tender, and I contemplate with anguish her having dedicated her life to a selfish failure. The reason for Martin's behaviour is that he is a bastard and clearly has a deeply-rooted resentment against procreation. You might say that Emma has a corresponding weakness of character in not having made him act more nearly according to her will. She would admit it, but she has made her choice. Perhaps neither she nor I ever wanted to be committed to relationships more critical and effective than ours actually were. Perhaps we are both too cautious. Now that my wife has been dead for over two years there is nothing to stop my making a determined effort to take Emma away from Martin, but I have not the strength or the will. We were never deeply or passionately in love, but we could have been had things turned out differently: 'Love me little, love me long.'

A period of extreme isolation began. I didn't see my friend Simon, my most intimate companion, very often during the years that followed the disaster with Celia. My wife and I lived on together in harmony, and the children grew up. My need for close relationships with young women did not disappear after Celia left me, but my attempts in this direction did not succeed, perhaps because I didn't really want them to. The need was still there, but my wish was to renew relations with Anne and live placidly. I made, as the opportunity arose, not very convinced passes at likely girls, with the results they deserved. I got nowhere with any of them. The girl I became most fond of was just going up to Cambridge. She had great sensibility, intelligence and humour, and we became friends. But she had no sexual interest in me, and when I kissed her and she saw that I had too intimate an interest in her (after all, I was married) she tried to end the friendship. On my promise of good behaviour, however, she resumed relations. Later she married a Cambridge professor. They and I are still friends. Harriet wasn't pretty, but she had a clear skin and a good figure. She also had a pretty speaking voice, and the sound of a voice is to me almost as much of a sexual attraction, or repulsion, as some other physical attributes. She knew, I imagine, that so far as sex was concerned I was philandering.

Harriet had a young brother, Justin, whom I also found attractive. Looking back on it, I can see that I was in a transitional phase between hetero- and homosexuality. This phase lasted for several years. I found young people of either sex attractive, but none compelled me to risk breaking again the order and outward harmony of my home. I had a profound compassion for Anne, who was certainly the only woman I could have made my wife and stayed married to—the only one, that is, who would have accepted me. But the need for physical intimacy and passion remained, though it was damped down. It was always acute at times of boredom or loneliness, and these were frequent. I was also going through a long period of self-hate and self-blame. All this combined to heighten my interest in something which had been latent in me from schooldays—the interest in flagellation. I brooded on this subject, discussed it whenever I got the chance, read about it as often as possible. When Anne was out of the house, the children were at school and I had the place to myself, I would strip myself in the large, warm living room (bedroom and bathroom were too small) and beat my bottom for as long as I could bear it. Then I would stand on a chair and look at the marks in the big mirror over the mantelpiece. I used a whippy switch cut in the garden or a short piece of clothes line. As I continued this practice until very recently, that is for about fifteen years, it clearly had some hold on me, and I will say something general about it here.

Everything about a whipping is sexually exciting, so long as it is done on the buttocks with a flexible object. To read about it is better than nothing. To see it done, as I have during my teaching days, is better; but I have never seen it done on a naked body. The contemplation of the stooping posture, as if in the attitude of a slave, is extremely exciting. So is the sound of the instrument as it whistles in the air and bites sharply into the flesh. The drawing of blood takes away from the aesthetic satisfaction of the beating. The groans of the victim and the sight of the raised weals are part of the ritual.

I did not beat myself regularly, but only when compulsion and opportunity coincided. The words would suddenly come into my mind: 'I'm alone this evening. Shall I beat myself?' Even if I tried not to, the compulsion that had put those words into my mind was too strong. I knew that I was to be the victim of my own sadism, that I must punish myself, and give myself at the same time the acute pleasure of sharp physical pain. As I have said, it has to be on the buttocks—I don't know why. I have discussed this with a friend of mine called David, and he agrees. We were introduced by some mutual friends, and later, when I met him by chance in a pub, there began a close though intermittent friendship. I found that David, considerably younger than I am, could be disarmingly frank, but as I came to realise how serious and reliable he was, I began to confide in him. I have often seen him in company, where he is lively and amusing, but I think his listening to me sprang from a genuine concern and yet gave him a vicarious pleasure. I was later to realise how far his interest in flagellation went. David agrees that a beating has to be on the buttocks. He has a sadistic but no masochistic interest in flagellation. He has never, so far as I know, had any desire to be whipped, though he told me he had once flogged a prostitute. The experience had been expensive and humiliating. It has been suggested that the buttocks resemble breasts, and that in this way whipping is a way of punishing some mother figure. I think it more likely that because the bottom is a very sexually attractive part of the body, near the most immediately sexual zone, and because the flesh there yields just the right amount to the imprint of the instrument, the aesthetic satisfaction of seeing or imagining a whipped bottom is keenest.

David asked me once why I beat myself. I said I didn't know, but that I usually associated it with boredom, unslaked sexual hunger and a fascination with pain in this particular form. An orgasm, especially a wholly satisfying heterosexual climax, is accompanied by pain. The point about both is that they are intense physical sensations. Boredom is a state in which we lack intense feelings, or feelings of any kind. A whipping, like a sexual experience, creates, at least for the time being, the feeling of being alive, rather than half dead.

One of the pleasures of beating myself was the feeling of tingling warmth which followed. Alas, it would disappear all too soon, perhaps because I didn't beat myself hard enough. I beat myself as hard and as long as I could stand. I would take perhaps a dozen, perhaps twenty or even more strokes, according to how well and strong I felt. When it was over, and I had groaned and become breathless, I would enjoy looking at the marks in a mirror and feeling them with my hands. It was of course a sad, self-hating business, serving only to heighten the loneliness of my situation. It was a secret, solitary *Schadenfreude*, sterile and unsatisfying, since it led nowhere and produced no lasting satisfaction. The only thing to do was to wait until I could stand it again.

I was discussing self-flagellation with David about five years ago, and I suddenly said: 'I'd like to be beaten by you.' 'Would you?' was all he replied. He was not sexually attracted to me, nor I to him. One evening, a year or two later, he was staying the night in the absence of my wife and children, who were on a short holiday somewhere. We had finished supper and had had at least a good bottle of wine between us, probably preceded by other drinks. Suddenly David asked! 'Would you like to be beaten tonight?' 'Yes,' I replied at once. It was settled. I had never been beaten by a friend or anyone else since leaving school. Celia had occasionally given me a stroke or two, but she did not like it, and in the hotels we stayed in, there was never anything better for the purpose than a wooden clothes hanger. David and I went upstairs, we both stripped and put on dressing gowns. Then David came into my bedroom and I took off my dressing gown and knelt over the bed in the posture of a slave ready for punishment. I felt a delicious sensation of ritual self-sacrifice. I had handed him the first weapon that came to hand, a short length of plastic-covered clothes line which I used on myself. The episode was not a success; we were both nervous. He was hurried and perhaps dared not strike as hard as I would have liked, nor was the instrument suitable. To be a success the act would have had to be more coolly planned and, the instrument better chosen. I told him he could give me eight strokes. He did so, too fast and without enough deliberation. I enjoyed it, but would have enjoyed it more if we had planned it more carefully. Then a strange thing happened, as unpremeditated on my part as it was unexpected by him. I seized him, opened his dressing gown, pushed him back on the bed and fumbled for his flaccid prick, which I pressed into my mouth. I didn't know why I was doing this, I only knew I had to. David was shocked and repelled. Next morning we were very subdued. The incident estranged us for a while, but the fault, if there was one, was mutual, and we acknowledged this. We have never repeated the incident or the assault. To find out about oneself, one must commit oneself to an action, and the result is often not very flattering to one's ego. From that time on, I stuck to auto-flagellation, tape-recording the sound of whipping, my groans and breath indrawn with pain, partly to gloat over myself in retrospect, partly to interest David.

12

The other element in my secret life which occupied me during these last fifteen years was the gradual loss of interest in girls and my growing attraction to boys and young men. The only woman I went to bed with, apart from my wife, was Emma, whom I saw secretly four or five times a year. Her gradual disillusion with her husband made her increasingly willing to be unfaithful to him, and one day she said to me, 'I was so fed up with Martin this morning that if I'd had you there I'd have slept with you.' This was invitation enough. Next time I went to see her I borrowed the key of a friend's flat. Emma and I had lunch. She was not free for long and after a hasty meal we went to the flat, switched on the fire, and I undressed first myself and then Emma. Her body was very beautiful, and she was warm and loving. But it was a chilly day, and we were not ready for sex. I didn't get an erection. We made one more attempt some years later, but the same thing happened. I realised that, unless I could enjoy the relaxation of sleep and a whole night in a warm bed, I was not likely to succeed. We never had the opportunity for this. Besides, although I love her as a person, and have done for sixteen years and more, and she is physically very affectionate, my sexual interest during this period has been increasingly directed away from women. I told her this, and she was always amused and sympathetic. I think she would make a wonderful wife or mistress for the right man but, as I have said, she has an insane loyalty towards her unworthy husband.

My growing desire for homosexual experience took several forms. I was by nature furtive, unwilling to commit myself; I didn't wish to reveal my propensity in such a way that people might gossip about me. I have never been able to throw off the deep-seated effects of my conventional upbringing. I would gaze hungrily at any male under the age of thirty or so with a clear skin and regular features—errand-boys, shop assistants, students, the sons of friends, fellow passengers in trains and buses, boys in the office, pictures of young men in illustrated magazines, particularly if they were partly naked. The thing built up to a smouldering fever, perhaps never to be slaked. What I wanted to do I did not really know. I was not particularly interested in normal homosexual perversion. All I wanted, I think, was the warmth and assurance of physical contact with young naked flesh. I wanted to possess young men, to kiss them, to share or to overcome my loneliness with them. I would choose a seat in a train next to or opposite some attractive boy and try to chat him up, always without any response from him except a polite willingness to talk. The loneliness of the human situation is something not confined to middle-aged men, and young men and boys also are ready to talk, if they don't think you have designs on them. I was, as I have said, a coward, unwilling to risk my pride in inviting humiliation. It seemed to me that I was doomed to enjoy the contact of these boys in fantasy only.

It was a constant pleasure also to touch boys and young men whenever possible—the hand of a shop assistant when I took the change, the shoulder or back of a clerk when passing him in the corridor. Gradually I became desperate, I realised that I must dare to do something active. I am not naturally impulsive and am incapable of taking some violent action by which I risk losing everything. This sexual timidity is fatal. Yet I suffered a morbid fear of being talked of behind my back, or of my wife and my growing children knowing me as a queer. I had been taught to shun and despise homosexuals, or at best to make a joke of them. I neither did nor do despise homosexuals. I think everyone should be happy in their own way, so long as they don't harm others. I know a number of homosexuals and bisexuals, and they are among the most sensitive and interesting people I know. Women friends usually say they like homosexuals because, being sufferers and, at least until lately, ostracised, they can sympathise with outcasts, the unhappy and the lonely. However, unless I went over openly to homosexuality—and how could I with a wife and children and some friends who would have been shocked—I was fated to be secretive, furtive and unfulfilled. I couldn't see that it was any worse to want to kiss and embrace a pretty boy than a pretty girl. Yet it was thought to be worse and, in some circles, unspeakable. Yet as I say, I began to feel desperate. I was middle-aged and feeling I would soon be old. A sense of approaching age is a strong inducement to overcome moral cowardice. One has less to lose, more to gain by boldness. All my efforts in this direction, limited as they were, were vain. I will recount a few.

Tom Blunt was a clerk in our office whom I would occasionally have into my room to go over some figures. He was not pretty, but he was well-made and fair skinned. We began to talk of his home background and his love of cricket. Perhaps he sensed sexual interest on my part. I have noticed from experience that when a young man is aware of this on the part of an older man, even if he has no homosexual tendencies that he would admit to, he will try, perhaps out of innocent vanity, to encourage that interest. He is a flirt, a cock-teaser. This is natural, and it flatters the older man. It does no harm, and if the older man is hurt, he has only himself to blame. I asked Tom if he had ever had homosexual experience. He said, 'Oh yes. When I was nine or ten, a schoolfellow and I used to play about with each other.' I asked if he was interested in flagellation, and he said no, but that once a man had asked him, when he was a boy of ten or so, if he would go for a walk with him and beat him with a stick and then masturbate him. Tom had declined. Then, in connection with his interest in cricket, though I'm not sure how the subject came up, he told me he had a very white skin. He was indeed red-haired, with face reddened from exposure to fresh air and fine weather. Such types often have very white flesh where it is not exposed. One day, inflamed by the thought of all this, I sat on the arm of his chair. It was a hot day, his jacket was off, and his flannel shirt unbuttoned at the wrist. I drew his sleeve up a few inches and gently stroked his lower arm, which was indeed very smooth and white. 'Are you like this all over, Tom?' I asked. 'Yes,' he said, and then added, rather stiffly, 'Do you mind not strokin' me, Mr Y.' He had a faintly Cockney accent. Rebuked, I instantly withdrew with a mumbled apology. He said in a bitter tone, 'I thought I had a friend, but I find I have a lover.' I didn't pursue the subject, though I could have pointed out that there is nothing incompatible between the two rôles.

Such humiliations were now common in my life—I was getting hardened to them. My next effort was with another young clerk, Daniel Amies, who had a very pretty face, long girlish eyelashes, high cheekbones, a charming and engaging manner, he was anxious to please and full of humour and intelligence. I never saw his small, neat, appealing figure enter my room without wanting to take it in my arms, I never did, though, and I helped him in his work and his problems with girls. He was frank. I was his confessor, and of course I got vicarious excitement from the recital of his adolescent problems. Though I had myself no active interest in girls then, I didn't in any way dislike them or shun hearing about sexual experiences. I suppose there was a father-son relationship between Daniel and me, for I felt I must advise and help him. His own father was buttoned up and severe, and Daniel couldn't talk to him. He told me that he was having a passionate affair with a girl, as it were on the rebound from a failed romance with another girl. They had gone together on a warm summer day to a secluded common and there stripped themselves naked. Daniel was sexually very excitable, as I afterwards learned, and the strain must have been considerable. At last the girl said, 'Take me.' Daniel refused. I wouldn't generalise, but I believe that girls are far more readier to lose their virginity than boys. I think, too, that it is the more responsible and intelligent among boys who have an instinct for preserving their virginity for what they instinctively feel to be a more real and fruitful relationship than any infatuation, however intense.

Of course I touched Daniel on every possible occasion, but it was his frank heterosexuality which made it unthinkable that I should try to persuade him to any kind of relationship with me. My friend Simon told me afterwards that I could probably have seduced Daniel, but I question this; and anyway, I didn't want to seduce anyone. I helped Daniel in every way I could and put him in the way of earning the money on which to get married to his wife Lucy, whom he loves and to whom he is now happily married. They are both my friends. I have kissed Lucy, who knows well how much I helped Daniel, and in her presence I kissed Daniel on the cheek for the first time. He is still the attractive, charming boy he was, and his affection for me has never changed. A year or so ago, when I was in deepest misery and dejection, I put my arms about his shoulders and, not long afterwards, told him of my plight. He said he had never guessed at my bisexual tendency until then. This shows how cautious I must have been, for I was certain that he could have guessed, had he wanted to. I am sure he has no homosexual or bisexual tendencies, and I didn't want a perverted or abnormal relationship with someone who had no abnormal tendencies, however attractive he might be. Daniel too, I think, unconsciously flirted with me, to gain the attention and notice of one whom most people respected and whom he knew not to be evil.

Mark Aston was a charming and attractive young man, anxious to get into shirt manufacturing. I happened to know a director in a firm in this line and introduced Mark. In gratitude the boy came and talked to me, and I became very fond of him. I let him into a good deal of my secret life, telling him of my loneliness and my interest in flagellation. I asked him if he would beat me. Without actually refusing, he never did, and he didn't care for me enough, or perhaps he cared too much, to do what would have been distasteful to him. We talked about music, in which he had a strong interest. I think he guessed at my homosexual tendency, but how could I interest him in it when he was undergoing an acute heterosexual crisis himself? So the pattern was repeated.

Another young man to whom I was attracted got help from me in exchange for his company and some other minor services, but without wanting to have me as a lover. I didn't blame either of these boys then, and I don't now. I wasn't bold enough, nor had I the opportunity, to find occasions when it might have been possible to seduce them by some active assault. Besides, I didn't want this; I preferred their good opinion and I detested the thought that they would talk about me and spread the idea that I was queer. So Mark Aston became a friend and, not long afterwards, a husband and father.

Justin Lane, the younger brother of Harriet, was dark, almost sallow-skinned, not conspicuously attractive, but he had good eyes and a nice smile. He had also a good body and a supple walk. He wore tight jeans. He was intelligent, though very moody and awkward in company. He was anxious for my companionship, he wanted my advice and sympathy. I saw little of him while he was up at Oxford, but occasionally we would meet in London and go to a pub and talk. On these occasions he always exasperated me by his opinionated talk and his egocentricity. But I was attracted to him and enjoyed his company at infrequent intervals, even while it somewhat repelled me. It turned out, moreover, that he seemed to have genuinely homosexual tendencies, though he was evidently worried by them and tried to combat them. He told me that he seemed to be able to make no progress with girls, but he valued the friendship of one or two male undergraduates. We didn't meet often, and after I had seen him I never made further attempts to meet him; it was he who always wrote and asked what I was doing and whether I would meet him.

After he came down we saw each other rather more often. He was desperately lonely, as any such awkward character is likely to be. I tried to point out his rudeness and how it repelled even me, who was pretty indulgent for the sake of his bright eyes, his charming voice (when he was not sulking) and his lithe figure. Once he invited himself to stay with me and my wife for the weekend. He came, and was as awkward and unsociable as ever. He used to go off by himself and walk about the streets, without any warning to host or hostess. On the Sunday we had two friends to lunch, an engaged couple. He took a violent dislike, as he afterwards told me, to the woman—a pleasant and attractive person whom it would have been difficult for any normal person to dislike. Immediately after lunch he disappeared to his room, packed his bag and left by train without saying a word. It is hard to explain this except by saying that Justin was evidently becoming increasingly psychopathic. I didn't see him for some time.

Then about four or five years ago I went through an intensely depressing period. Combined with my increasing desperation about ever finding an outlet for my homosexual feelings, which seemed to be eternally fixed in a pattern of furtive and unsuccessful overtures to attractive but uninterested young men, I was once more under sentence of a possible second operation. The state of mind of someone awaiting the doctor's verdict about an internal operation can never be cheerful. It is at times like this one wishes one were a cheerful extrovert. I began to think more and more about Justin. Was he not, by admission, at least a potential homosexual? Was he not himself lonely and in need of sympathy? Surely he must have some sympathy for me. It was only later that I learned at first hand of his psychopathic narcissism, his constitutional incapacity for feeling for anyone but himself. He was an interesting case, as I was to find out. He may indeed have tried to understand and to sympathise with me in my trouble, but he was no more able to do this than most stone-deaf men can appreciate a symphony. We would meet from time to time for a coffee or whisky. He would talk about himself or about indifferent things. He had little interest in me. I would try to put my hand on his shoulder or his knee, or to touch his hand. If I succeeded, he silently withdrew. Although he didn't seem to want my attentions, I think he was flattered by them, and perhaps the idea of encouraging the attentions of someone he liked and respected began to appeal to him. He became more confidential. I told him frankly of my interest, and he told me that he could never become emotionally involved with anyone except small boys of pre-pubic age. I think the psychologists recognise this type as a paedophiliac or something of the sort. Justin took every opportunity of playing village cricket with little boys or amusing his nephews and nieces by playing games with them. I feel sure he didn't interfere with them sexually, or physically in any way. He collected pictures of small boys and began to take an interest in pop stars, whose pictures he collected. When one of us went abroad we exchanged postcards. His were usually views or old masters—he had very good taste. I sent him from Naples a photograph of a charming naked little boy on a fountain—a classical statue, for nudes are not sold openly.

That autumn I saw him again. He told me he had a new flat, a self-contained bedsitting-room which was very reasonable. He had a job in a printing firm, which paid him well but not lavishly. He was by this time about twenty-three. He said he would meet me and take me back to his room, where we could talk more easily than in a pub. I was in a very emotional state, in despair about my life and deeply apprehensive about my health. Something had to be done. I determined that I would make a pass at Justin, if there was the slightest chance. I put a bottle of whisky in my briefcase, knowing he would be unlikely to have any in his room. I was full of guilt and self-reproach, but there seemed to be no choice. He led me upstairs, and I took in his room. It was small but had a pleasant view over a backyard with trees; it was very quiet. There were bookshelves, a gas-fire, chairs, a table to work at, a cupboard and, against the back wall, a single bed. The bed was clean and on it was a pair of clean pyjamas. Two chairs were placed close together. On the mantelpiece he had ranged a row of picture postcards. One of them was the naked little boy I had sent him from Naples. One was Elvis Presley. We started talking. 'Would you like a drink?' I asked. 'There's some whisky in my case.'

He said he would, and I poured out two sizeable shots, which we topped up with water. We drank in all perhaps half a bottle between us.

His right thigh was very near me. I put my hand on it, and he took my hand in his. Gradually his thighs opened a little. I didn't really know what to do. He was in his gayest and most attractive mood. Time passed and I said, 'I think I ought to get the next train. I'll take a taxi.'

'Why?' he asked.

'Well, Anne will be expecting me,' I answered. 'I didn't say I'd be back late.'

'What are you afraid of,' asked Justin, taunting me.

'I don't know.'

'Well, stay.'

An hour later I decided I must go. It was true that I was always careful not to leave Anne later than she expected. If I stayed the night with Justin, I could of course ring up and say I had met an old friend and gone back to his home for the night. But I thought I had made good progress with Justin, and I didn't want to lose the advantage I thought I had by being precipitate. In this I realised later that I was mistaken. Had Justin wanted, he could have made me stay.

'I really must go,' I told him. 'Shall we meet this time next week?'

He agreed, and I said I would get a taxi to his flat and come up. He was full of charm and complaisance, appearing very reluctant that I should go. I picked up my coat and my briefcase, and he went to the door to let me out. He smiled warmly, and I said, 'Kiss me, Justin.' He shook his head gently and said, 'No.'

For the whole of the next week I thought of him. I was in an agony of fear, doubt, expectancy, hope. Was I at last going to achieve what I had tried for for so long without success?

When, the following week, I visited Justin's flat for the second time, he didn't answer the street door bell himself. His landlady let me in. I found my way up to the third floor. He knew I was coming and when, but he wasn't out on the dark landing to greet me. I knocked at his door, and he said 'Come in.' He was sitting at the table, writing. He didn't get up. The room was very differently arranged. The two chairs were as far apart as possible. There were no pictures of boys on the mantelpiece. There were no pyjamas on the bed. Instead, there was a guitar, making it impossible to sit there without moving it. We sat on the two chairs. I asked him if he would like some whisky. I got up and put my hand on his shoulder. He freed himself and refused a drink.

'Is anything wrong?' I asked.

'Yes,' he said. 'I didn't like the way you behaved last week. What did you mean by producing whisky like that?'

'You didn't have to have it,' I replied. 'I didn't think you would have anything up here to drink. You've only just started in this job and have the flat to pay for. We could have met in a pub, but you wanted me to see the flat. I like to offer my friends a drink.'

After we had talked for a while I left. I said I would ring some time, and perhaps we could meet in a pub. He agreed. His manner was cold.

I felt very wretched, I was worrying about my health and he knew this. I was also in a fever over my emotional problem.

I rang him two or three weeks later. It could not have been sooner. He agreed to meet me at a pub we had often been to before. I was there on time. An hour later he had still not arrived and I decided to catch the next train home. I rang up his flat, and he answered.

'Hullo,' I said. 'I'm at the pub. You said you'd be here by six.'

'I know,' he said. 'I couldn't come.'

There was no word of excuse or apology.

'I waited,' I said.

'Yes, I thought you might.'

I rang off and went for my train.

That was the last I saw or heard of him for three years. I would gladly have left it at that. One reason why I had continued to meet him from time to time was that I had promised his mother I would. She always worried about his instability. She need not have worried. He always looked after himself, since that was what he lived for. He would always fall on his feet. Indeed, there was something feline about him. A year later (I am anticipating in order to round off the story of Justin) my wife died, and his mother must have told him, for some months later he sent me a note of sympathy. He gave me his number at his new job and asked me to ring some time. Months later I rang, thinking it might be interesting to see him again. After all, my life had utterly changed and, although my emotional problem was still unsolved and I was in a state of despair I no longer had any intention of trying to become intimate with Justin. We met at the same pub where I had waited vainly for him before. It was convenient for my train home. Justin had put on weight and was now rather prosperous. He didn't ask much about me, but was eager that I should know how he had fared. He told me he lived in a different flat above two friends, a married couple. He was fond of them both. I asked, in the course of our conversation, if he had yet lost his virginity with either a woman or a man. He said he had not. He was twenty-six, and knowing how I had felt at that age in the same situation, I could not help sympathising. I thought I might visit him, but I would like one thing cleared up first.

'You stood me up last time we were going to meet,' I said.

All he replied was: 'Yes, I remember. I thought you deserved it.'

And with these words in my ears I said good-bye and went. I have not seen or heard from him since, and I hope I never shall. I have thought a lot about Justin, and of course I blame no one but myself for my involvement with him. It takes me a long time to become disillusioned about someone in whom I have invested some affection and regard and to whom I have given some help and sympathy. I don't want thanks, because thanks come from the heart, and Justin had no heart. He was cold, and coldness is something I can't accept from anyone. It comes from a total lack of humanity, of understanding for anyone but one's self. He was the perfect narcissist. His relations with me were never spontaneous on his side, never natural. I had always put this down to his being psychologically tied up. He spent some money in going to psychologists, with what result he never told me. Such visits were perhaps no more than a way of spending money on himself. We all do that, particularly when we were sorry for ourselves. But I hadn't realised until long after my first two visits to his flat that our relations were not only not spontaneous, but were in fact on his side contrived and calculated to the last degree. He was not a fool and had got a good degree at Oxford. He had done everything necessary to encourage my advances. Of that there could be no doubt. Before my first visit I had made it quite clear that I was interested in him as a lover. The reader may wonder why he wanted to encourage the advances of a man more than twice his age when he could have had younger men for the picking, if he had wanted them. I was not unknown in my profession, and had the reputation of a man of some distinction. My interest in Justin flattered his vanity and gave a sadly needed lift to his ego. But he didn't really want intimacy with anyone of either sex, young or old—except with the little boys he knew he could not have. It is a terrible thing to have an exclusive infatuation with one's self.

13

During and after the attempt on Justin I was going through the most miserable and desperate period of my life. I was getting on for sixty, worried about my impending operation and in a fever to fulfil my ambition to have a homosexual relationship before I was too old. I began to feel more and more driven to make overtures to any young man with whom I came into contact and who attracted me. During all this period my friend Simon was immensely helpful and sympathetic. He never lost interest. He was one who cared about anything in which he was interested, and he had always been concerned for me in the twenty years of our friendship. I asked him if he supposed it was possible for a young man to be attracted to a man twice his age or more. He said he didn't know. We agreed that there seemed to be no homosexual equivalent of the girl gerontophile. My lack of attraction to women continued, and I was as passionately obsessive about boys as I had been about girls in my Celia phase.

I was on my way to stay with Harriet Lane in Cambridge and was taking my seat in the dining car when I saw a personable young man by himself at a table for two. I asked his leave and sat down opposite. It turned out that he was the football correspondent of a London newspaper. He also told me in the course of conversation, when the subject of families came up, that he was 'a bachelor'; he didn't simply say that he wasn't yet married. I thought afterwards that it was an odd thing to say, unless he was hinting that he was a homosexual. I was ignorant of the language of homosexuals, who I imagined must have a lingua franca. He also told me that next week about the same time he would be in Cambridge. He was, I recollect, going to Newmarket or Norwich—somewhere beyond Cambridge. But if this was a hint, I didn't take it. It would not have been easy for me to get away from my host and hostess in any case. The young man and I had not drunk enough to talk without reserve. That was that. I didn't see him again.

I considered how best to make contact with any men I knew to be homosexual, so that, if possible, I might get a footing in their society. There were said to be homosexual pubs in London. I went into one on one occasion, but I saw no sign of anything or anyone that had anything remotely suggestive. Perhaps I had come at the wrong time of day. Then I heard casually that there were homosexuals to be found in Carnaby Street. I walked slowly down it, keeping my eyes open and wondering what I should do if the opportunity arose. A young man in a white shirt and jeans was standing outside a door. He wasn't very attractive, and his face was slightly pitted. Beside him stood another man dressed in just the same way. He was stouter, thickset and had, when I got close enough to see clearly, the most repulsive face I have ever seen. He had thick, very sensual lips, narrow, hard eyes and a sallow face with scars. He asked me aggressively what I was looking for. I felt an instinctive fear and said, I don't know why, 'It's all right. I'm friendly. Is there a pub near here?' The thug directed me, while I glanced at the boy. If he was a male prostitute, I couldn't imagine going to bed with him.

I can't remember all the other casual, abortive attempts I made. I was afraid I might do something dangerous—it was before the time of the 'consenting adults' law. I read with fascination the newspaper sensation of the wretched trade union official who had enticed an Irish boy to his flat, made a pass at him and been killed by being hit on the back of the head with a bottle of whisky. I read all I could get hold of, including a moving account of a boy in South America called Manuel, imprisoned for killing an elderly seducer with a brick wrapped up in brown paper. I read later *Last Exit to Brooklyn*, which I found deeply moving as well as horrifying; the whole subject was horrifying in its grimmer aspects. There was the terrible episode in the newspapers of the nobleman and the boy scouts, and then there was the well-known actor caught soliciting by a police trap. I read also the life of the poet Housman, being especially moved to compassion at the fate of Oscar Wilde in the nineties. One was still affected, even in the middle sixties, by the contempt with which many people spoke of queers. It created a climate of opinion, ordinary middle-class opinion, in which a tendency even to bisexuality was necessarily a guilty secret. I was with a friend of mine in Rome, and a pretty, mincing, dark boy came into the café where I was chatting with the proprietor and a few friends. They shunned the boy, who seemed not to mind, and whose manner made it quite clear that he was a homosexual. He was very merry and, I thought, attractive in a roguish way. It seems that on the Continent, at any rate in Italy, a queer is a queer, without concealment. When he had minced his way out of earshot, the proprietor's daughter said in tones of utmost scorn—she spoke good English, and I had no Italian: 'That filthy queer! He thinks he's Cleopatra.' I thought I should not in the least have minded making love to him, and how that would horrify my companions. I didn't see him again. They told me there were a lot of queers in Rome. This of course is to be expected in a country which guards its young women so jealously.

It was decided that I was to have an operation. There was no immediate hurry, and a bed was booked for me in a London hospital for October. This decided, my wife and I were then free to go on holiday. We arranged to fly to Greece in September. Made morbid by my plight, I was prepared to go to almost any lengths to gratify my festering desires. I had heard something of the reputation of a men's outfitter who kept a shop near where we lived. I had bought things from his shop, and had been served by him over the counter. His face was repellent, with its sharp nose and near-set, beady eyes. But he was neat and clean, always polite and anxious to please. Local queers used his shop, I think, as a meeting place. His name was Jack, and he was notorious for trying to get off with the young men who came to try on clothes. A young man of my acquaintance told me with amazement that he had never been quite so openly manhandled while being fitted for a suit. All this aroused my curiosity and interest.

One day I went in to buy a pair of trousers, a light-weight pair suitable for going abroad to a hot climate. 'Like to try them on?' asked Jack. 'Put them on in there. I'll be in shortly.' He ushered me into a curtained cubicle, and I put on the trousers. When the man came in to see how they fitted, he fumbled with my genitals, though not in a way which, if I had violently objected, could have been taken exception to. I imagine that when this was done to a strict heterosexual, the customer simply did not come back, but had a laugh with his friends over it. I bought the trousers and went out.

A few days later I said I wanted some underpants. 'Try them on if you like,' said Jack. I shut myself in the cubicle and stripped naked. Then I put on the pants. Jack was delighted and immediately embraced me and took out his enormous prick with great dexterity. His wife was serving in the shop at the time. She was an attractive-looking woman, younger than he was, and I couldn't help wondering if she knew all about her husband. Jack's prick, now erect and huge, was thrust into my hand. I pulled him towards me, doing what I supposed I was expected to do, but without excitement, only a kind of experimental fascination. Homosexual experience could be as passionless and strictly sensory, I concluded, as heterosexual experience was said to be with a whore. Indeed, Jack was no more than an amateur male whore. I thought about him. There was nothing in him to be harsh about or to take a high moral tone over. He was very kind and performed a useful public service. I was considerably older than he was; he must have been in his early or mid forties. He had black, well brushed hair. The only thing against him was that he was a coarse man and physically repulsive. I went into his shop again at what I knew to be a slack time for business. His wife wasn't there and I said I would like to try on a shirt. He had said, 'Come in any time and try something on. There's no need to buy anything.' Once more I stood naked, waiting for him to serve a customer who had just come into the shop.

Over the curtains of the cubicle I heard him trying to get rid of the customer without losing his professional politeness. At last he returned, opened his trousers and embraced me, rubbing his hands up and down on my nipples 'Oo!' he said, smacking his lips. 'Lovely!' I put my hands into his trousers and over his smooth bottom, pressing him up against me. I had no erection. His was enormous. I took it in my hands and gently massaged it, loathing the whole business, as a young man loathes his first impulsive experience with a prostitute.

'We could have fun,' said Jack, Whereupon he thrust an enormous, gleaming tongue deep into my mouth. It seemed as large and gristly as his prick. I was revolted, since this is a form of intercourse I don't much enjoy, even with someone I love. Then a customer came in, and I said I had better get dressed. I did so, and when I emerged from the cubicle, the shop was empty once more.

'I don't want to be seen,' I said. 'Of course not,' he replied. 'I have to be careful too, you know.'

An ironical factor in the situation was that the police station was only a block away. From the curtained window in the cubicle one could see the men as they went on or off duty. How the detectives would have enjoyed themselves if they had known what went on behind the small curtained window a few doors off. When we were alone, I talked for a while with Jack. 'You've a very nice wife,' I said. 'You're not a hundred per cent.' He looked puzzled and then said: 'Oh, I see what you mean. No, I like the best of both worlds.' He spoke with a coarse, North Country accent. 'I could come up to your place when your wife's out,' he suggested. 'I could bring some patterns along. It's quite normal. 'My wife's usually at home,' I said cautiously, 'but I could let you know.'

In my fantasy I saw myself rolling about on a bed with Jack, both of us naked, he perhaps buggering me. The thought was horrible. I felt mean to be so revolted by him, because in reality I felt a kind of humble gratitude. It wasn't his fault that he was revolting. I told him that I was going abroad the following week, but that I'd be in touch.

This experience was traumatic for me, and it was only by

discussing it with Simon that I found relief from the sense of nastiness and despair it brought me.

Two days later, almost on the eve of our intended departure for Greece, I was rung up by the police. I was told that my wife, driving back alone from visiting her sister in the Midlands, had had a serious accident and was in hospital. I hurried to her side. She had no chance, they told me. And indeed she never regained consciousness, which was a relief in a way, and she died that night in my arms. No one who has not had this experience can understand the sense of shocked unbelief that I felt for weeks and from which I have never wholly been freed. I still address comments and asides to my dead wife, and confide in her.

The crash hadn't been her fault, the police told me; it had been a head-on collision with a skidding lorry. In grief and anguish I returned home, having made the necessary arrangements, and cancelled the trip abroad. I never ceased to regret that she had died without our having had the chance of that reconciliation I so deeply desired. We were in a sense reconciled, for after the Celia affair I never again gave her cause to worry about the stability of our home. She was a good wife and, above all, a great companion. We had in common all that really mattered most in life. As for me, there was no reconciliation and nothing to look forward to but an operation to improve the health I no longer desired to preserve, except for the fact that the pain was intolerable. An operation seemed to me only less intolerable than the worst pain it was intended to prevent.

I didn't go and see Jack again for many months. Then at last I felt I owed it to him to say something. He had done me no harm and only wanted to exchange with me what he regarded as pleasure. 'Sorry I've not been in,' I said. 'We never went to Greece. My wife was killed in a car crash.' 'Oh, I'm sorry,' he said with true sympathy. 'Since then I haven't felt like anything of that sort.' He understood. Not long afterwards he left the district, I don't know why, and we didn't meet again.

14

My operation, carried out a few weeks after Anne's death, was pronounced to be successful. I had a fortnight's convalescence to fill in—reading, getting out of bed and regaining my steadiness in walking. Friends came to see me, especially in view of my recent bereavement. As everyone knows who has been in hospital, life there becomes something on its own, highly concentrated and, as it were, cut off from the outer world. The personnel who have to do with patients—doctors, nurses, cleaners—take on the rôles of entirely new *dramatis personae* in one's life. There is an air of unreality, or super-reality. Left alone a good deal of the time in my small private room, I began to realise the full impact of my bereavement and to reflect once more on my wretched situation. I heard from one of the nurses, a day or two before I was to be discharged, that a young Yugoslav occupied the next room to mine, waiting his time for an operation. He had come over specially from Belgrade, because this was the best hospital in Europe for his particular operation. His father must have been comfortably off. He could not, I was told, speak a word of English. I imagined he would be lonely and decided to call on him, take him some of my superfluous fruit and see if there was any language in which we could converse. I could manage German, French, or Spanish at a pinch. I knocked on his door and went in.

'Hallo,' I said, handing him some grapes on a plate, 'would you like these?'

He smiled and took the grapes but said nothing. He was sitting up in bed in his pyjamas. He had no need of a dressing-gown: hospital rooms are always too hot. He was listening to light music on a transistor radio but he switched it off as I sat down on the one chair the room offered. 'Do you speak English?' I asked. 'Deutsch? Español?' To all these he shook his head. I then found out that he could manage French. He spoke with a very bad accent, bad grammar and scanty vocabulary, but we achieved a surprising degree of conversational exchange. As we talked I looked at him. At first I thought he was plain to the point of ordinariness. Then as I watched him more closely, I realised that his face, foreign and presumably Slavonic, was one of extraordinary charm, even beauty. He was very fair-haired, with short, blond curls. His skin was of a great delicacy, pale cream, smooth and almost transparent. His eyes were black and brilliant, but almost closed by the slit-like shape of their openings, pushed together, as it were, by the height of his cheekbones. His mouth also was almost a slit, wide when he smiled. His nose was straight, his features regular and almost classical in a Balkan way. In retrospect I thought of his face as one of the most individual and beautiful I had ever seen. His father, he told me, was in London while he was having his operation. The young man, whose name was George (or whatever is the Yugoslav equivalent) was in his early twenties. He had no other visit than the daily one from his father, and no one in the hospital he could talk to. So he was glad, I thought, of my interest. He was a gay, sport-loving boy, probably of no great depth, who played pop music when at home. He played the guitar, he liked rowing and was in some team. He had a sister who spoke much better French, he told me, than he. He was a student, but I forgot what he told me about his proposed career. Then I had to go and have my lunch, and I said I would come back later. I did so in the slack period between afternoon tea and supper.

This time I sat on his bed. I felt an overwhelming desire to touch him, so I put my hand gently on his shoulder. He made no objection and after a bit he pushed back the bedclothes—it was still too warm in the room—and swung round to sit beside me. With my left hand I slowly unbuttoned his pyjama jacket, murmuring something foolish in French, like 'Vous permettez?' He was perfectly passive. I couldn't tell if he welcomed the attention or not. He certainly showed no embarrassment or distaste. I put my hand round his side to his back, feeling his smooth, warm flesh with a hesitating delight. I pulled him gently towards me and kissed his cheek. What he was thinking I couldn't imagine. After that there seemed nothing else to do: I could hardly start an affair on the last day of my stay in hospital with a young man awaiting an operation. A nurse might come in at any moment. Perhaps I had an idea we might start a productive friendship. I asked him if he had a photograph. He got off the bed and fished one out of his wallet and gave me it. He also gave me his address in Belgrade. It was exactly like a friendship on board ship, quickly begun and destined to wither. I told him that, if he were ever in England, he must get in touch with me. We might meet, and perhaps he could stay with me in the empty flat. We probably had very little in common. However, for the moment he seemed a wholly delectable change from the misery of my life. George and I exchanged letters, short and in bad French, after he had returned home. I learned afterwards, to my relief, from an actor whose acquaintance I had made, himself an active homosexual who had money and travelled a good deal, that love-relations are common between men in Yugoslavia. They are, I gathered, of the bisexual kind. There doesn't exist there (or indeed anywhere, I believe, except in the Anglo-Saxon world) that complete taboo on close male friendships which so arbitrarily divides the normal from the perverted in our puritan minds.

Next morning I went to bid George good-bye and good luck. I took him the still fresh flowers that had been given me by friends to brighten my hospital room. He was delighted. I shook hands with him but I didn't touch him apart from that. For a long time I mourned the ineffectuality of our meeting; it seemed to have followed the usual pattern of such episodes in my life.

Gordon Marshal was the son of an old business acquaintance of mine who had died some years before the boy first came to see me. His mother had thought I might help him in setting up in business on his own. We had met for a drink some time before Anne's death, and he had struck me straight away as very attractive. He was then living outside London, and I didn't see him often. After Anne's death we became friends; he had taken a small flat of his own and was freer to meet me. We talked about life and literature and about Gordon's business hopes. He had great charm of speech and manner. He was kind and sympathetic to me in the loneliness of my bereavement. He was short, neatly and lightly built, with small hands and feet and his hair was smooth and dark. His skin was good, inclined to a high colour on his cheeks, though whenever he was tired or unwell the colour drained. His eyes were brilliant, dark and prominent, his cheekbones high, his mouth full and clearly defined. His nose was straight and almost prominent—it was a very determined, handsome and characterful face and he readily attracted people of both sexes. His cool beauty, ease of movement and quiet liquid voice made his presence immeasurably comforting. The outcome seemed inevitable considering my state of mind at the time. Yet I don't know if I would have made any move had he not actually made it for me. Looking back, I am sure he did it intentionally.

Gordon must have guessed my interest in him. One evening we were sitting close together in a pub. There were few other customers at the time, and our position was secluded. After a few drinks the subject of bisexuality came into the conversation. It was natural—he was just down from Oxford, and homosexuality was very much in the air. Then he stopped, looked me in the eye and said coolly: 'Are you bisexual, Richard?' I paused. Then I said: 'Since you ask directly, yes. But I don't talk about it. I'd hate the children to hear.' 'Of course,' he agreed. I never heard that he gave me away to anyone, though he told me his friends suspected that I loved him. 'I am too,' he said.

I don't think this was strictly true, though he may have thought it was at the time. In the three years I've known him I have never noticed the slightest evidence of anything in Gordon but avid and normal heterosexuality. I told him about my feeling for him, and he said he had guessed.

Probably I was not the first, for he knew how, as they say, to look after himself. I drew my chair very close to him and, as we stretched out our legs in front of us, I pressed my right leg against his left, from hip to foot. He made no move either to get closer or to withdraw. I made furtive approaches to him in this way each time we met in a suitable place. I took to resting my hand on his thigh. Sometimes he would take it, but he always prevented closer intimacy.

As the months passed, my fever of infatuation grew. I saw him as often as I could, and he didn't abuse his power over me to cause me any unnecessary suffering. Once I lent him money, but it pleased me to do this. I had a mild martyrdom complex where love was concerned. It was all part of the pattern which I had come to regard as my life style. Beauty was unpossessable, love unattainable except on the rarest occasions. I suffered, but it was a bracing, almost exquisite suffering which was infinitely preferable to boredom and the aridity of being without desire. 'It is better to have loved and lost . . .'

Being in love, or thinking one is in love—how it gives new life to the old platitudes. I did in any case enjoy Gordon's company. He was an amusing companion, always considerate of my feelings. If he didn't want to go to bed with me that couldn't be helped. I think, now I recollect our meetings, that with some determination and perhaps some experience I could have seduced him. He once told me that I was too hesitant, too furtive—I should be bolder, more positive, more active. But when I tried to be, he evaded me, and I felt humiliated. Shortly after I declared myself for the first time, I said to him: 'You know my feelings for you. Do you mind? Would you rather I tried to suppress them?' 'No,' he answered in his level way, 'I don't mind.'

One difficulty I had was the consciousness of my own age. Even though I had homosexual leanings myself, I couldn't envisage a single man over twice my age whom I would have liked to make love to me. I assumed that the young are just not interested physically in the middle-aged, and that was that. I longed for the miraculous encounter, but it had not come, and I despaired of its ever coming.

Not only did Gordon show no signs of bisexuality, as I have said, he began to show a marked interest in fast girls, verging on the nymphomaniac. He introduced me to two of them, and they were very agreeable. I chatted them up openly in front of Gordon and one of them made a pass at me when Gordon brought her to my flat one day. We got slightly drunk—indeed, perhaps I was more than slightly drunk—and we sat together on the sofa, with me in the middle. I put my arms round both of them and tried to get inside their clothes. The girl's seemed to be sewn together. I got my hand inside Gordon's shirt and ran my hand over his smooth side and breast. I must certainly have drunk more than I remember, because I can recollect suggesting we all three went to bed together. They were not drunk enough for this, and both firmly declined. Later they went to bed with each other.

As time went on, Gordon became very occupied with his business ambitions, and I saw less of him. He brought an Australian girl over to see me. He had picked her up in Hampstead and he said they had spent the following three days in bed together. She was like his previous girl—pretty enough in a superficial way, easy to get and easy to get tired of. I was in an emotional state over Gordon and did a bit of desultory necking with the girl. Later she tried to get to know me better, but I had no interest in her. On almost the last occasion when I had a drink with Gordon, he had, without consulting me, invited the Australian girl. She joined us and we had drinks. The Gordon said he had an engagement for dinner and left me with her. I found it quite hard to shake her off. I don't hold anything against Gordon, but I couldn't help feeling hurt: it seemed as if our friendship was ending. I had asked for what I got, and my hurt was caused by my usual mistake of idealising the object of my desire. It's a hard world. Don't come into the kitchen if you can't stand the heat. I romanticise and I pay for it. Perhaps it's better to stick to plain sex, obey the rules and try to hurt no one. Lust is pure, and love is a mess. I dedicated myself then to friendship, the death of love, the heart's despair, the atrophy of feeling.

15

I write the final chapter of the story of my emotional life in my sixtieth year. It is, in some ways, the most amazing. I must say something of my state of mind at the time I met Julian, who was then twenty-two. I had, as I have related, attempted to become intimate with a number of young men, but without any success—indeed, with a good deal of shame and humiliation. It seemed as if the fever of this phase had abated, and I had relapsed into a dull but not unresigned despair. I knew now that I would never have the relationship I wanted. This experience, I felt, would have rounded off my life and given me the complete range of emotional experience of which I was capable. But this was not to be. If it should arise of its own volition, so to speak, so much the better. But it must come just like that, not through any humiliating efforts of my own. I wanted it most fervently, but the fervour died and the desire atrophied. If something should reawaken it to life, well and good. Gone were any thoughts of trips to countries such as Denmark and North Africa, where young men were said to be available for the picking. Gone were chattings-up in trains and pubs. That was all finished. The image of myself as an ageing, balding man of near sixty, with a lined face and something of a paunch, haunted me, and the idea of this man furtively seeking contact with people of the same sex and no more than half my age sickened me. The account of what followed may indeed sicken some readers. I can only record it as it happened.

Julian worked in the same block of offices as myself and lived with his widowed mother a street away from my flat in outer London. Since my wife's death nearly two years earlier, my life had gradually sunk into an uneventful but not discontented regime. I had plenty to do, plenty to worry about, relatives to see and to help. But I lived more or less by and to myself, apart from the presence at eight in the morning, before I left for work, of an agreeable, middle-aged domestic help. She cleaned the place, looked after the laundry and sometimes prepared meals. It happened that Julian and I often found ourselves travelling home by the same tube or bus. If it was wet, I sometimes took a taxi, which I invited him to share. He did this readily and without embarrassment or suspicion. He had no cause for embarrassment, for I had no particular sexual interest in him. He didn't attract me at first, though I imagined in a general way that his slight and boyish body might be beautiful. He showed no outward sign of any great distinction, but his speech was good and his manner pleasant, unaffected and respectful. He talked to me freely, without subservience or familiarity. We spoke of what are called indifferent topics—the weather, the news, foreign countries he had visited with his mother. We also talked of books, music, theatre, films, art, in all of which we had interests in common. He had had a good education at a big London day school and was well-informed on many things, so that our conversations were always a pleasure to both of us. I took to asking him to my flat on his way home, to talk or read me something he was interested in, or just sit by the gasfire if the evening was cold. I would give him a glass, or at most two glasses, of sherry and a cigarette or two. At first he stayed only for a short while, then a little longer—up to an hour or more. I had ruled out all thoughts of trying to seduce Julian. I was not, in fact, anxious to do so. I was too fond of him to run the risk of his displeasure and disillusion. When I say he was unaffected, I mean something more positive than that. He had a natural wish to please and to be liked. If I ever asked him to do me some small kindness—to fetch a book, go to the pub for cigarettes, or whatever it might be—he did so just as if it was his place to do so, but without excessive deference. I was the provider and the man of sixty, he was the young friend of twenty-two.

I found out that Julian's mother knew he visited me and

didn't object. I had met her in fact on occasion at the local pub, and I found her sensible, intelligent and cultured—almost, indeed, the predictable parent of Julian. She accepted me as a friend for him and perhaps as the counsellor whom most young men need. He was taking an exam for further qualifications and I was able to help him.

Julian came to my flat once or twice a week. I got to know him better, and I found him to be an introspective boy, very lonely and frustrated. His was not an uncommon case, and it was very similar to what mine had been at his age. This drew us together. Then when I asked him, as one does in a general way, how he felt, he began to tell me how bored he was, and how stale his office and his exam work had become. He felt adrift in a world which didn't understand him. I would never have found this out had I not questioned him, and after all, even at my age, I felt much the same. Loneliness can draw people together.

One evening I gave him a cigarette and offered him some white wine. He accepted and I had a glass too.

'Bored?' I asked—'Same as usual—life flat, stale and unprofitable . . .?'

He nodded and drank more wine.

'Haven't you a girl friend?' I asked, anxious more to understand and help him than to introduce myself into his affairs. The question opened the floodgates.

'No', he said. 'That's the trouble. My friends say I must be queer, but I'm not. I just don't think anything of the girls I know. If you meet them at a party, all they want is to go the whole way at once. That's not what I want.'

He spoke, not nervously or with any hysteria, but with quiet self-knowledge and a rueful smile which I found charming. If he was something of a prig he was no more than I had been—less in fact. He didn't disapprove of other people's conduct; he simply knew that sex for its own sake was not what he wanted. What he needed was the intimate companionship of someone who would trust and understand him and talk to him. I told him that perhaps he had had bad luck with the girls he knew. They were not all nymphomaniacs, I imagined, and somewhere there must be a girl with something to give him other than her virginity. But there is among many girls, as a result of emancipation and what might be called the sex explosion, a readiness to dash into bed with a man the first time they are with him, and they seem ignorant of the fears of sex which a sensitive boy feels, ardently though he may desire it. They are unaware of the strength of masculine pride, the nervousness in the face of their own bodily powers and functions. Such a boy needs patient care and understanding, perhaps from an older woman. A girl of seventeen, even one of fourteen, may be sexually more mature than a boy of her age or much older. Julian told me that the girls he knew, while sexually precocious, were emotionally immature.

I asked him if he had had any homosexual experiences. He told me he had had an affair six months before, now coming to an end, with a cousin of his two years older than he. They had been to bed together on many occasions. I asked if they had practised buggery.

'Yes,' he said with vehemence. 'It was horrible. I hated myself for doing it and I hated him for making me.'

Together we finished the wine; we were talking freely and without restraint. It was past the hour when he usually went home, but I didn't notice the time. We went into the kitchen together, I forget why, but I think it was to get something more to drink. We had drunk just enough to make us talk without inhibition, but without lack of control. We were standing very close. I faced him, and as he stood in front of me, a little taller and considerably slimmer, he looked enormously appealing and in need of comfort. I could do no other than put my arms round his shoulders. He had on a thick navy-blue sweater over his shirt and I could feel his firm shoulders underneath. Julian at once put his arms round me. We held each other very close, and he began swaying passionately backwards and forwards, I going with him. As we stood locked together in the kitchen, Julian said softly to me, in a tone of intensity, the four words: 'I love you, Richard.' For years I had heard nothing that moved and delighted me more.

We went back into the living room and fell into each other's arms on the sofa. I don't remember that we kissed each other. He simply clung to me as closely as he could, while gradually my hand went down to his waist, and I pulled up his shirt at the side and felt for his body. Its smoothness, suppleness and warmth gave me intense pleasure. I had found something I had been looking for as long as I could remember. The contact of his young, lithe body assuaged a deeper thirst than any wine.

As we half sat, half lay on the sofa, Julian clinging to me tightly as I embraced and caressed him, I was in a daze of incomprehension—I cannot remember what I said. He told me that I understood him and he needed me. I told him I needed him no less. We stayed like that for longer than I realised, for in the end his mother rang up to ask if he was with me. He rearranged his clothes and left. I heard him answer his mother very coolly on the telephone, saying we had talked, and then I had needed help with some work. It was nearly ten o'clock. I spent the rest of the evening alone in a state of euphoric disbelief.

For the remainder of that week there was no chance of seeing Julian again as I had to go to Manchester on office business, so I told him to call on me after breakfast on Saturday. He had spent Saturday morning with me on two or three previous occasions, so there would be nothing unusual in that.

On my journey to the north and for most of the rest of my time I had nothing to do but to think of the boy. Now that the impossible had happened so suddenly, without premonition or premeditation, I was nervous, worried, excited, almost afraid. My conscience told me to beware of confirming him in a homosexual tendency which both of us deplored. Yet I was sure he wasn't homosexual: he had told me so during our long conversation. He said he looked forward to marriage and children, and that the affair with his cousin was no more than a substitute for the heterosexual relationship which he couldn't achieve with any girl he knew—or any woman either. I thought I was perhaps something like a combination of father-figure and father-confessor. Nevertheless, the extreme physicality of his feelings towards me amazed me to the point of disbelief—there must be a mistake, soon I should wake up. I determined that as soon as we were alone once more, we should go to bed together. There was no other possible outcome. Then I began to fear that he might have second thoughts and would not come. If so, there was no help for it. He must choose; I could not persuade. I have been to bed with four people during my life—I didn't have to persuade any of them. I have tried to persuade others, but without success. What must be must be, so I spent the rest of the week dreaming of the astonishing good fortune which had fallen to me as a recompense for the years of loneliness, shame and frustration.

Julian's appearance was not in any obvious way striking; no one would have singled him out in a crowd as a beautiful boy. Nor would anyone have singled him out as in any way ill-made or unattractive of feature. He had had his hair cut too short, but it was beginning to grow again and give a little weight to the upper part of his face, which was on the narrow side. His profile at close quarters was attractive—regular, clear-skinned, almost pretty when illuminated by pleasure, as it usually was. It was an intelligent face, and for me intelligence, which also includes humour, always has its beauty. It could have been the face of a girl but for the shaven chin.

Nothing could have convinced me, if I had needed convincing, more than my knowledge of Julian, of the polarity of the sexes. Julian was a man, first and last, but his feminine qualities (what we call feminine) were present in his nature and character. He loved the world of art and all aesthetic sensations; he was gentle and hated violence. He told me later that the one thing that had always made him lose his temper was the attempt by anyone to dominate him by force. I imagine he could be very stubborn and angry. At the same time he had masculine caution and shrewdness, consistency and perseverance, level judgement and a certain realism not inconsistent with idealistic, even romantic tendencies. He was attracted to members of his own sex, but had had no relationship with anyone but his cousin. His hands were beautiful and might have been those of a girl; they were very gentle. As I came to know Julian and his hands well, I knew, if I had not known it before, that hands are as much an indication of character and temperament as are faces.

When Saturday came I had breakfast early and cleared the things away. No one ever visited me uninvited on Saturdays. We were sure to have the flat to ourselves. My state of nervous excitement was indescribable. All I could do, after I had put on the electric heater in the bedroom, was to walk up and down. Exactly at ten, as arranged, the door bell rang. Julian, who stands straight, with a slim grace which is very touching, walked straight towards me after closing the door, and our arms were round one another.

'You haven't changed?' I asked.

'No,' he said coolly, 'but I don't want it to go too far. I don't want to be too involved.'

'Nor do I,' I reassured him.

I took him by the hand and led him into the bedroom. Mine was a single bed, but wide enough for two. 'Put your clothes there,' I said, indicating a chair.

We undressed together in silence. Then we stood together, naked. His prick was already erect, the top covering his navel. For him, as for me, the act of undressing in the presence of a lover was a ritual in itself sexually stimulating. I had no erection, which I ascribed to my being in my sixtieth year. We put our arms about each other, and Julian began to breathe deeply, sighing uncontrollably. At first I didn't touch him below the waist—not with my hands, that is, though I felt his warmth and the pressure of his prick on the front of my body. Then we moved to the bed and got in under the covers. It was too cold to be completely uncovered. We put our arms round each other. It seemed like a new life to us both, or at least the death of something unspeakably dreary and sterile.

I was reminded then of Celia's words some eighteen years before. 'Be careful what you want. You are sure to get it.' I had longed for Julian's love and desire for years before I knew him, and here he was to fulfil my longing and my need. We loved one another because of our mutual need. I had not fallen in love with Julian for his face, though I came to love it as the most sensitive and expressive part of his body. The lack of conventional beauty of face in Julian made the shock of his bodily beauty more intense. It gave me immeasurable joy. Julian was slim—almost too much so, we agreed. His proportions weren't classical, and there was not, for aesthetic perfection, enough flesh on his legs. But he was truly graceful, supple and flexible. His skin, smooth and without a lot of hair, except on his legs below his hips, was cream-coloured, with almost no white and pink. To stroke him endlesly from his neck, down his chest and belly to his too slim bottom, became my greatest pleasure. I never tired of it, and it delighted him to be caressed. I loved kissing his shoulders and arms—his face too and his mouth, though with less purely sensual pleasure because of his shaven chin. I loved, too, running my fingers through his brown hair, and later I grew to be fond of his sinuous, hairy thighs. Our warmth and sensuality gave us untold pleasure.

At first we were shy, but the shyness didn't last long. I told Julian truthfully at first that I was not interested in his genitals. I had always in fantasy ignored the genitals of males, which, as with women, do not strike me as aesthetically attractive but simply functional, receptive or aggressive as may be. There is something very tender about the thought of a loved one's genitals, but that is not the same thing as aesthetic beauty. It soon became evident that to ignore Julian's long, thick sexual organ, consistently in a state of excitement, was impossible. After we had lain and embraced for some time, I put my hand on his prick and said: 'Hadn't we better do something about this?' I was not particularly anxious to masturbate him, and it was certainly not something I would ever persuade him to, if he were reluctant. We had no thought of anal coition, which he said was horrible, and which I imagined would be painful to us both. Julian said 'Yes', and I began gently to masturbate him. He became increasingly excited and jerked his prick up and down in my hand. He asked me to hold it lower, which I did. I was myself circumcised and was not familiar with the feel and shape of an uncircumcised prick. His foreskin was always getting in the way and being crushed. I am told that circumcision reduces sexual pleasure, but there is no means of knowing. As he grew more excited, he said: 'Do you want me to go all the way?' 'If you want to,' I said. I have never thought that an unfinished act of masturbation is any good. It's always finished off afterwards in private anyway, and I couldn't bear the thought of Julian's going home to masturbate by himself in his room or in the lavatory. So I got out a clean handkerchief, and he ejaculated into it. He then became quite passive, satisfied and breathing deeply. He was always aroused quickly after we had stripped and embraced each other, I only slowly. As he became more passive and dreamy, I became more active, stroking and caressing every part of his body, to our mutual delight. We got out of bed after an hour, I knelt at his feet, put my arms round his waist and buried my face in his belly. I was still, and for some little time afterwards, shy of paying much attention to his prick, but eventually I became fascinated by it and loved it as the organ of his highest sensual enjoyment. I envied him its size and alertness, but I expect mine had been the same at his age. I was unwilling to let him dress again, but we put our clothes on, tidied the bed, lit cigarettes and went into the kitchen to make coffee. Then he read to me, and we talked, and I sat beside him on the sofa and laid my head in his lap and took his beautiful cool hands in mine. After an hour or so Julian went home, but not before we agreed that our love must be a complete secret. We would meet again casually and come back to my flat together three days later.

I was still unsure of him. I thought he might regret our behaviour and leave me. I was prepared for this—it would hurt, but by my time of life I had been through so much disappointment that I was hardened to it. I need have had no fear. He always came promptly and eagerly, as anxious as I to assuage the thirst that had built up in the interval. The next time we once more went straight to bed. This time he was very active and passionate, wholly male. I was deeply gratified by his passionate behaviour, his attempt to treat me as if I were a woman. 'You'd better try coming between my legs,' I told him. When we had arranged a towel beneath us, and he had found the right position, I squeezed his hard organ between my thighs near the top, and soon he came. It gave him intense satisfaction, and I was happy in his satisfaction. We then lay still for a time, until presently we were excited once more and twined our legs together in an effort to get as close to each other's nakedness as possible. This time the room was warmer, and, without entangling sheets, we enjoyed each other's bodies to the full.

'I didn't feel at all guilty after last time,' Julian said.

'Nor I,' I said, but I think he was nearer the truth than I. Even so we never once so much as attempted to bugger each other. He was of a new, 'permissive', amoral generation, but I had been brought up by a father who only once referred to Oscar Wilde's trial, and that with horror, and by a mother who knew only in theory, if she knew at all, that the horrors of homosexuality existed. What Julian felt about our relationship was instinctive; what I felt, which was the same, had something of an intellectual conviction in it. I can only say that, whatever my afterthoughts, I was conscious, when with Julian, only of the innocence of our love. We were not depriving someone else of it nor hurting anyone else. He was not a child—everything we did together was natural and happy. All sorts of burdens, nervous and psychological, had fallen from our shoulders, and we walked as free and innocent men. Julian told me that his work had improved, and later that he had found something that was tangible and that he could grasp. It was as if his experience had at last caught up with his thoughts. 'Now the world is a real place to live in,' he said. 'Before, it was a region of vague sensations and unrealised conceptions.' Everything else had fallen into its proper place and proportions for him. Anyone who has enjoyed happy love knows this. He knows too that, whatever may be the ultimate outcome, this love is timeless. If true love dies, it is as a flower, natural and without final remorse.

But we thought nothing of the future until one day, a week or so later, Julian told me that he had been chosen as one of several in his firm to go to South America in a few weeks' time as part of his training. He said this quite lightly, but not casually or heartlessly. He never had it in him to be heartless. I knew that he had to go if he was chosen, it was part of his career. I had already told him he must be considered first, because he was more important than I, simply by virtue of his having more of his life before him. He went out of the room for something, and when he came back I was sitting on the sofa, apparently looking unhappy.

'Why are you looking so unhappy?' he asked, in evident surprise.

'Because you're going away,' I said. 'I can't help it.'

He almost laughed, saying gaily:

'But it's only for nine months.'

I was infinitely touched by his youthful faith in his own faithfulness. As to this, we made each other no promises, needing none. Tacitly we agreed to enjoy the weeks ahead.

We never had a moment's unhappiness together. We never quarrelled or rebuked each other; we had perfect mutual trust. I told him that if he found someone he preferred to me (for I had to own to myself that there might be many other possible lovers more suitable than I) he was not to hesitate to tell me. He said, 'That's very generous of you.' He never took advantage of our changed situation, since becoming lovers, by asking from me anything he would not have asked before. 'I always admired and respected you,' he said, and I was grateful, though I am still a little embarrassed by anything said to me which sounds like flattery. He told me that every time we met I said something that made him love me more. I loved him more and more, the more intimate we became.

Our meetings were always happy, and we had more lighthearted than serious talk, though we had that too. We went to bed together for an hour or more each time. I can't describe each encounter in detail. Once I said, 'let's not masturbate today.' Julian agreed, but before long he became so passionate and excited that it seemed like cruelty to keep to our resolve. 'I'll have to come,' he said. 'It's no good.' So I took his prick in my hand and did as he needed. The passions of the young are compulsive. I couldn't be so insensitive as to have forgotten the torture in youth of unslaked sexual desire. He liked best to lie on my chest with his legs each side of my body and fuck me between the thighs, as nearly as possible as with a woman. On such occasions he was usually very aggressive, and we clutched and clawed at each other with fierce tenderness. Once he said, as we got into bed, 'I'm afraid I'm not feeling very active.' Soon afterwards he became as excited and passionate as ever and fucked me with the same fervour as before. Afterwards I said, 'I thought you weren't feeling active. I'd like to have you when you are!'

I enjoyed taunting him, and he always responded with feminine delight, but we never flirted or played tricks on each other. I taught him to play with my genitals, as I did with his, but he was always shy of starting. But to give him pleasure was no self-sacrifice to me—I loved it as much as my own pleasure. It *was* my pleasure. I tried to get him to hurt me, explaining that I was naturally masochistic, but he didn't want to. He bit me lightly sometimes, as I bit him, but he hated pain and giving pain. I had no desire that he should beat me. If he had any sadism in him I should have enjoyed it, but it isn't natural to want an unwilling flagellant as a lover. Our love was always gentle, not violent. I think I am now past the need or desire for violence. Since we became lovers, I have given up both self-flagellation and masturbation. He loved having his slender, feminine waist gripped between my legs until it almost hurt. I had no desire to exploit my influence over him by learning with him any unnatural perversions. I was so wholly fulfilled with what we had that I didn't want to give way to greed for what we had not. I think this was true of Julian too. We didn't talk much about our love, except in the immediate physical context; we didn't worry it to death with self-analysis and self-examination. It was perhaps, to some extent, an experiment in extroversion by two natural introverts. This was what made it so delightful and so satisfying. I was always satisfied, to whatever extent is possible in such a love, by an hour or two in bed.

We were temperamentally so well suited, so matched in our

mutual need, that we never tired of each other. Julian always stayed as long as was prudent, sometimes a little longer. On one occasion, when I got him to come three times in one week, he said his mother had remarked on it, though without suspicion, and he would not come more than twice next week. I always respected his feelings and wishes when I knew what they were. He never said or did a thing which caused me annoyance or cast a shadow on my feelings for him. He was sensitive and fastidious, whether in bed or out. I promised not to write to him at home or ring him up there. His mother believed I was helping him with his studies, as I was, in so far as love-making allowed. He also helped me, a lonely widower whose children were able to come and stay only at infrequent intervals. All that he did which beguiled and pleased me, all his warmth and charm, humour and sensibility seemed so spontaneous and natural that I never discovered whether any of it cost him any effort. Even standing upright takes an effort, after all, but you see no sign of it. I wanted Julian only to be Julian, and being oneself is not effortless for a person with sensibility and ideals.

Often when I was alone in the evenings, I was seized with loneliness—always a form of self-pity—and wished to have Julian with me. He told me it was the same with him. The result was that, when we did eventually come together, we couldn't wait to make love. I was of course tempted, in fantasy only, to make him read or talk and smoke, so as to see if he would make me go to bed. But it isn't in my power to have or to want to have that kind of power over anyone. Besides, perhaps I should have failed. He knew that if he didn't feel like making love I wouldn't make him. To some people all this may sound cool and prudential—what has love to do with prudence after all? It would take too long to answer this. I can only say here that there are as many kinds of love as there are different people, and Julian and I were true to our own and each other's natures. To be otherwise would only bring misery and remorse. There is enough of that.

The reader might wonder why I have written of this experience in the past tense. How did it end? What happened next? It didn't end, and nothing happened next. As arranged, Julian went off to South America—for six months, not nine as originally planned. We loved each other as much, and more, when we parted as when our love began. We had quite a gay parting, getting up and putting on our clothes for the last time with a kind of ritual slowness of leave-taking. We made no promises, not even to write, but we knew each other's addresses. I don't allow myself to hope. I have suffered too much in my sixty years to indulge in the dangerous fantasy of counting blessings that I neither have nor have as yet had. Perhaps I am cured of fantasy. I haven't written to Julian, as I can't let myself come between him and any other experience he desires or needs, even by a letter. He hasn't written to me, but he has been away only six weeks. Instead, I have written this account of my life, and I shall show it to him. Is it fantasy to dwell on the happiness he has so lately and so unexpectedly brought me?

Some may think this is a mere sentimental infatuation. I know it is not. Some might say it is merely a willed realisation of some long felt desire hitherto unpersonalised. All love is to some extent that. But it is nonetheless personal. What matters in love is the gradual, or even sudden, realisation that the object of one's love is the coming to life of an idea—in Plato's sense—which had existed in the soul long before. I know Julian well enough to know that he is that—the other half of the egg. Shall we one day find out that we were not this to one another, and that to believe so was an illusion? If so, it was—it is—worth it.

'If you doubt it,' perhaps you, my dear Julian, will say when you read this, 'how can you think you love me?' How can I know, my dear? As between innocence and experience, however, innocence is infinitely more wise, more endearing, and more fallible. It is also more vulnerable, and I can't endure to wound you with any false ideas of mine. Is our love a mutual infatuation? Is it a 'marriage of true minds', as you called it? Is it no more than impassioned physical affection, based on mutual sensuality, need and hunger? Perhaps it is all these, as love can be. But to try to define love is to get farther away from it. We can be sure of it only in action. I love you for your physical affection, intelligence, sensitivity, kindness and tenderness to me, and for the beauty and sweetness of your young, warm body, which I picture in my mind till my eyes smart with nostalgia—nostalgia for a lost island, for an island not yet reached. Let me not, at any rate in your absence and through the thought of you on the other side of the ocean, inflate our love into something it is not. The lesson of life is to face the facts—facts about others, ourselves, the world. If this is not a consuming, romantic passion, we are the better for that. Perhaps you will have that one day. Perhaps I am too egocentric ever to have had it. All the same, I would do a lot for you. I told you once that I couldn't help feeling gratitude, and you said you hoped it was not that. So I amended what I had said to: 'Well, then, I am grateful *for* you—for the fact of you, your existence.' I said I only wanted you to be you. I hope you always will and that it will not be too painful for you to find yourself. Now that you have read this, if you think I make too much of our love, that is an old mistake of mine. My mistakes are me, just like everything else. The question is, I sometimes think, what else have we to live with but our mistakes?